Giving Up the
Ghost

Giving Up the *Ghost*

(A MEMOIR)

HILARY MANTEL

A JOHN MACRAE BOOK
Henry Holt and Company   New York

Henry Holt and Company, LLC
Publishers since 1866
115 West 18th Street
New York, New York 10011

Henry Holt® is a registered trademark of Henry Holt and Company, LLC

Copyright © 2003 by Hilary Mantel
All rights reserved.
Originally published in a slightly different form in
Great Britain in 2003 by Fourth Estate, London.

The lines from "Sharecropper's Grave," by Judy Jordan, are published
by kind permission of the author and the Louisiana State University
Press.

Library of Congress Cataloging-in-Publication Data
Mantel, Hilary, 1952–
    Giving up the ghost : a memoir / Hilary Mantel.— 1st ed.
        p.   cm.
    "A John Macrae book."
    ISBN 0-8050-7472-4
    1. Mantel, Hilary, 1952–   2. Novelists, English—20th century—Biography.
3. Chronic pain—Patients—Great Britain—Biography.   I. Title.
PR6063.A438Z467 2003
823'.914—dc21
[B]   2003047757

Henry Holt books are available for special
promotions and premiums.
For details contact:
Director, Special Markets.

First American Edition 2003

Designed by Paula Russell Szafranski

Printed in the United States of America

1   3   5   7   9   10   8   6   4   2

For my family

Small holes, secret graves,
Children scattered around the iron fence.
Not even a scratched stone.

The wind rises, clouds cover the moon,
A dog's bark and those owls,
Alone and no end.

My children who won't hear.
The night full of cries they will never make.

"Sharecropper's Grave"
Judy Jordan

Giving Up the
Ghost

A Second Home

It is a Saturday, late July 2000; we are in Reepham, Norfolk, at Owl Cottage. There's something we have to do today, but we are trying to postpone it. We need to go across the road to see Mr. Ewing; we need to ask for a valuation, and see what they think of our chances of selling. Ewing's is the local firm, and it was they who sold us the house, seven years ago. As the morning wears on we move around each other silently, avoiding conversation. The decision's made. There's no more to discuss.

About eleven o'clock, I see a flickering on the staircase. The air is still; then it moves. I raise my head. The air is still again. I know it is my stepfather's ghost coming down. Or, to put it in a way acceptable to most people, I "know" it is my stepfather's ghost.

I am not perturbed. I am used to "seeing" things that aren't there. Or—to put it in a way more acceptable to me—I am used to seeing things that "aren't there." It was in this house that I last saw my stepfather, Jack, in the early months of 1995: alive, in his garments of human flesh. Many times since then I have acknowledged him on the stairs.

It may be, of course, that the flicker against the banister was nothing more than the warning of a migraine attack. It's at the left-hand side of my body that visions manifest; it's my left eye that is peeled. I don't know whether, at such vulnerable times, I see more than is there; or if things are there that normally I don't see.

Over the years the premonitory symptoms of migraine headaches have become more than the dangerous puzzle that they were earlier in my life, and more than a warning to take the drugs that might ward off a full-blown attack. They have become a psychic adornment or flourish, an art form, a secret talent I have never managed to make money from. Sometimes they take the form of the visual disturbances that are common to many sufferers. Small objects will vanish from my field of vision, and there will be floating lacunae in the world, each shaped rather like a doughnut with a dazzle of light where the hole should be. Sometimes there are flashes of gold against the wall: darting chevrons, like the wings of small quick angels. Scant sleep and lack of food increase the chances of these sightings; starving saints in Lent, hypoglycemic and jittery, saw visions to meet their expectations.

Sometimes the aura takes more trying forms. I will go deaf. The words I try to write end up as other words. I will suffer strange dreams, from which I wake with hallucinations of taste. Once, thirty years ago, I dreamed that I was eating bees, and ever since I have lived with their milk-chocolate sweetness and their texture, which is like lightly cooked calves' liver. It may be that a tune will lodge in my head like a tic and bring the words tripping in with it, so I am forced to live my life by its accompaniment. It's a familiar complaint, to have a tune you can't get out of your head. But for most people, the tunes aren't the prelude to a day of hearty vomiting. Besides, people say they pick them up from the radio, but mine are songs people don't really sing these days. Bill Bailey, won't you please come home? Some talk of Alexander, and some of Hercules. My aged father did me deny. And the name he gave me was the croppy boy.

Today, the day I see the ghost, the problem's just that my words don't come out right. So I have to be careful, at Mr. Ewing's, but he understands me without any trouble, and yes, he remembers selling us the cottage, seven years ago, is it really so long? They were years in which perhaps half a million words were drafted and redrafted, seven and a half thousand meals were consumed, ten thousand painkillers (at a conservative estimate) were downed by me, and God knows how many by the people I'd given a pain; years in which I got fatter and fatter (wider still and wider, shall my bounds be set): and during seven years of nights, dreams were dreamed, then erased or reformatted: they were years during which, on the eve of the publication of my seventh novel, my stepfather died. All my memories of him are bound up with houses, dreams of houses, real or dream houses with empty rooms waiting for occupation: with other people's stories, and other people's claims: with fright and my adult denial that I was frightened. But affection takes strange forms, after all. I can hardly bear to sell the cottage and leave him behind on the stairs.

Late in the afternoon, a migrainous sleep steals up on me. It plants on my forehead a clammy ogre's kiss. "Don't worry," I say, as the ogre sucks me into sleep. "If the phone wakes, it will ring us." I knew the migraine was coming yesterday, when I stood in a Norfolk fishmonger choosing a meal for the cats. "No," I said, "cod's too expensive just now to feed to fish. Even fish like ours."

I hardly know how to write about myself. Any style you pick seems to unpick itself before a paragraph is done. I will just go for it, I think to myself, I'll hold out my hands and say, *c'est moi*, get used to it. I'll trust the reader. This is what I recommend to people who ask me how to get published. Trust your reader, stop spoon-feeding your reader, stop patronizing your reader, give your reader credit for being as smart as you at least, and stop being so bloody beguiling: you in the back row, will you turn off that charm! Plain words on plain paper. Remember what Orwell says, that good prose is like a windowpane. Concentrate on sharpening your memory and peeling your sensibility. Cut every page you write by at least one third. Stop constructing those piffling little similes of yours. Work out what it is you want to say. Then say it in the most direct and vigorous way you can. Eat meat. Drink blood. Give up your social life and don't think you can have friends. Rise in the quiet hours of the night and prick your fingertips and use the blood for ink; that will cure you of persiflage!

But do I take my own advice? Not a bit. Persiflage is my nom de guerre. (Don't use foreign expressions; it's elitist.) I stray away from the beaten path of plain words into the meadows of extravagant simile: angels, ogres, doughnut-shaped holes. And as for transparency—windowpanes undressed are a sign of poverty, aren't they? How about some nice net curtains, so I can look out but you can't see in? How about shutters, or a chaste Roman blind? Besides, windowpane prose is no guarantee of truthfulness. Some deceptive sights are seen through glass, and the best liars tell lies in plain words.

So now that I come to write a memoir, I argue with myself over every word. Is my writing clear: or is it deceptively clear?

I tell myself, just say how you came to sell a house with a ghost in it. But this story can be told only once, and I need to get it right. Why does the act of writing generate so much anxiety? Margaret Atwood says, "The written word is so much like evidence—like something that can be used against you." I used to think that autobiography was a form of weakness, and perhaps I still do. But I also think that, if you're weak, it's childish to pretend to be strong.

Sell Owl: the decision came with us, crawling through the Friday evening traffic on the M25, and navigating the darkness of Breckland settlements with their twisted pines and shuttered houses. We had done this journey so many times, looping past the center of Norwich on the fringes of industrial estates, slowing at the crossroads among West Earlham council houses: lamps burning behind drawn curtains, no one in the streets. As you cross the city boundary the streetlights run out, the road narrows. You creep forward into that darkness which is lit only by the glittering eyes of foxes and farm cats, punctuated by the flurry of wing beats and scurrying of busy feet in the verges. Something unseen is eating. Something is being consumed.

As you enter the small town of Reepham you turn by the church wall, bashed and battered by many long vehicles, into the marketplace empty of cars. The King's Arms is still burning a light, the big doors of the Old Brewery are closed and its residents padding upward to their beds. Turning uphill from the square, you park on the muddy rutted ground at the back of the cottage, unloading in the dark and mostly in the rain; your boots know the puddles and slippery patches, the single dark step and the paving's edge. Sometimes it is midnight and winter, the cold sucking the virtue from a torch beam, diffusing the light into an aimless dazzle. But just as feet know the path, fingers know the keys. Fifty yards from the Market Place, there is no light pollution, no urban backwash to pale the sky; no flight path, no footfall. There is starlight, frost on the path, and owls crying from three parishes.

You sleep well in this house, though if you are here on a week-day morning the trucks and tractors wake you at dawn. Their exudates plaster the roadside windows with a greasy, smearing dirt. The country is not clean or quiet. Through the day hydraulic brakes wheeze as truck drivers come to a halt at the bottom of the hill, at Townsend Corner. But when they say town's end, they mean it. Beyond the police station, beyond the last bungalow—that is to say, in less than a quarter of a mile—the town becomes open fields. The next settlement is Kerdiston. Its church fell down several hundred years ago. It has no street names and indeed, no streets. Even the people who live there aren't sure where it is. Its single distinguished resident, Sir William de Kerdeston, moved to Reepham after he died, and lies in effigy on his tomb, resting—if that is the word—in full armor and on a bed of pebbles: his shoulder muscles twitching, perhaps, his legs flexing, every year as we reach the Feast of All Souls and the dead prepare to walk.

When we bought the cottage it had no name or history. It was a conversion of buildings that might once have been a house, or not; most likely it was some kind of agricultural storeroom. At some point early in the 1990s, a Norwich builder knocked four flats and two cottages out of its undistinguished structure of old red-brown brick.

In the winter of 1992–93 we were scouring the county for a weekend place. We went to the coast and deep into the heart-land, always keeping in mind the long journey from Berkshire and our need to settle, for weekends, close to my parents, who had retired to Holt. Studded into our Barbour raingear, driving our scarlet BMW, we were a sight to gladden the eyes of any country estate agent. We would see their faces light up, only to assume their habitual gray glaze when we introduced them to our stringent budget and our high requirements. We wanted nothing tumbledown, nothing picturesque, nothing with a small but containable dry rot problem. And nothing too remote, as I might want to stay there alone, and I am myself too remote and nervous and irritable to drive a car. We wanted a shop and a pub, but most Norfolk villages are straggling depopulated hamlets, with a telephone box, if you're lucky, to mark their center. All the same, we thought there was a home for us somewhere in the county. I'd just won a book prize, so we had unexpected cash to pitch in. Norfolk wasn't fashionable then. People thought it was too far from London, and it didn't have what urbanites require, the infrastructure of gourmet dining and darling little delis; it had pubs that served microwaved baked potatoes with huge glum portions of gravy and meat, and small branches of Woolworth in small towns, and Spar groceries in larger villages, and waterbirds, and long reaches of shingle and sea, and a vast expanse of painter's sky.

By this stage we knew Norfolk fairly well. I had first come to the county in 1980, to stay with friends who were themselves newly settled in a Broadlands village. My own home was in Africa, but my marriage was breaking up. A wan child with a suitcase—an old child, at twenty-eight—I went about to visit people, to stay for a while and drift away again, ending up always back at my parental home, which was then still in the north. I seemed to be perpetually on trains, dragging my luggage up flights of steps at Crewe, or trying to find a sheltered place on the windswept platforms of Nuneaton. As I traveled, I grew thinner and thinner, more frayed and shabby, more lonely. I was homesick for the house I had left, for my animals, for the manuscript of the vast novel I had written and left behind. I was homesick for my husband, but my feelings about my past were too impenetrable and misty for me to grasp, and to keep them that way I often began and ended each day with a sprinkling of barbiturates gulped from my palm, washed down with the water from some other household's cup. When you take barbiturates at night your dreams are blank and black, and your awakening is sick and distant, the day in front of you like a shoreline glimpsed from a pitching ship. But this is because you need some more. After an hour, you feel just fine.

My Norfolk host was a woman I had known in Africa. Her husband was working abroad again, and she didn't like to be alone in the country dark. If our strained expatriate lives had not brought us into contact, we would never have been friends; after a while I realized we weren't friends anyway, so I got on a train in Norwich and never came back. But our long drives about the county, lost in winter lanes, our limp salads in village cafés, our scramblings in overgrown churchyards, and our attention to the stories of old people had made me think deeply about this territory, and want to write a novel set there. After some years, this was what I did.

We had been separated for no more than two years when my ex-husband came to England, changed. I believe people do change; there's no mileage, really, in believing the opposite. I also had changed. I was living alone. I was sick with a chronic illness, swollen by steroid medication, and a cynic in matters of romance. Of Freud's two constants, love and work, I now embraced just one; I was employed six days a week at two ill-paid jobs, days in a bookshop and nights behind a bar, and I got up at dawn to write my journals and stabilize my body for a venture into the world. I kept notes for future books; at that time, 1982, I had published only one short story. I had given up barbiturates. I don't remember exactly when I stopped, or what I did with the endless supply of tiny pills from the big plastic tub I'd brought from Africa. Did I tail them off? Stop them cold? I don't know. In view of the claims I will later make for my memory, this causes me concern. Perhaps they brought their own oblivion with them, each rattling little scoop of pinhead-sized killers. Since then I have always been addicted to something or other, usually something there's no support group for. Semicolons, for instance, I can never give up for more than two hundred words at a time.

Whether I was fit, that summer, to make a rational decision—well, who ever knows about that? It seemed that what I had left, with my ex-husband, was more than most people started with. So we got married again, economically, at the registrar's office in Maidenhead, with two witnesses. It was September, and I felt very ill that morning, queasy and swollen, as if I were pregnant; there was a pain behind my diaphragm, and from time to time something seemed to flip over and claw at me, as if I were a woman in a folktale, pregnant with a demon. Nothing, except for having to get married, would have got me out of bed, into my dress, into my high heels, and into the street. The registrar was kindly, and wished us better luck this time around. There was no ring; as the size of my fingers was changing week to week, I didn't see the point, and it is possible, also, that I didn't want to resume the signs and symbols of marriage too quickly. We had lunch in a restaurant in Windsor, in a courtyard overlooking the river. We had champagne. A witness took a photograph, in which I look hollow-eyed, like a turnip lantern. This is how—I have to shake myself to say it—I have been married twice: twice to the same man. I always thought it was a film-people pursuit, or what peroxided football pool winners used to do, dippy people destabilized by good fortune. I thought it was what people did when they had stormy temperaments; it was not an enterprise for the prudent or steadfast. Though perhaps, if you're prudent and steadfast past a certain point, it's the only reasonable thing to do. You would go on getting married and married to that person, marrying and marrying them, for as many times as it needed to make it stick.

In mid-January 1993 we made our headquarters at the Blakeney Hotel, a flint ship sailing the salt marshes. We were equipped with sheaves of property details, most of them lying or misleading. For two days we drove the lanes, crossing houses off as soon as we saw their location or exterior. I was recovering from a bad Christmas—bronchitis and a lung inflammation—and I had no voice. But voice was not necessary, only an ability to peer at the map in fading light and at the same time monitor faded fingerposts, leaning under the weight of Norfolk place-names. At five on a Sunday afternoon, in near-dark, we were up to our calves in mud somewhere east of East Dereham, a stone's throw from an ancient crumbling church and a row of tumbledown corrugated-iron farm buildings, trying to find a track to a forlorn little cottage at the end of a forlorn little row. We gave it up, sat disconsolate inside the scarlet monster, and turned our minds to the M25.

When we returned, still in bitter weather, I had got my voice back and we had narrowed our search. Often, when I was staying with my friend from Africa, we had come to Reepham to shop, and I had looked up at the long Georgian windows of the Old Brewery. It was a pub and small hotel, an elegant redbrick building with a sundial and that Latin inscription which means

"I only count the happy hours." By the time I returned there, ten years on, Reepham had a post office, two butchers, a pharmacy, as well as a telephone kiosk: a hairdresser, one or two discreet antique dealers, a busy baker's shop which sold vitamins and farm eggs and organic chocolate, and a greengrocer-florist called Meloncaulie Rose. A well-arranged town square was surrounded by calm, wide-windowed houses, and a jumble of cottages tumbling down Station Road. There was no longer a station, though in Victorian times there had been two, and twelve beer-houses, and a cattle market. There had been three churches, but one of them burned down in 1543 and was never rebuilt; the history of the town is of a slow decline into impiety and abstemiousness. On a January day, after I became a resident, a huddled old lady beckoned me from her doorway and looked across the deserted Market Place to the church gates. "What do you make of it?" she said. "More life in the churchyard than in the street today."

The people of Reepham and the surrounding villages gather in the post office on a Saturday morning. They discuss rainfall—"not enough to wet a stamp," I once heard a man say. They talk about whether they have put their heating on, or switched it off, and about nonagenarian drivers who crawl the lanes in their Morris Travellers. They are not inhospitable. They don't make a stranger of you till you've lived there for twenty years. They don't in fact make much of you at all. People once employed on the land are now quite likely to work at a computer terminal. They don't know you, but they don't mind that. They're live and let live. They used to greet each other with "Are you all right?" a question with a unique Norfolk inflection, but they don't do that so much as they did. They go into their houses early on Christmas Eve and lock the doors. They leave their windfall apples and overproduce of vegetables outside their doors in baskets, for anyone to take, and sell bunches of daffodils for pennies in the spring.

When we went to see the house, the builder's debris was still in it. We stood in its unfinished rooms and imagined it. We imagined it would be ours. It was cheap, and a minute from the Market Place. At midnight, we left our room at the Old Brewery and walked to the gate: or to where the gate would be. We wanted to see it again, in privacy and silence. As we stood, hunched into our coats on a night of obdurate cold, the tawny owl called out from the tree.

Later we had a plaque made to say "Owl Cottage," with a picture. But the man did a barn owl, canary yellow and thin, with creepy feet like the feet of a rodent.

It's a strange phenomenon, the "second home." Like the second marriage, it's not something that I ever associated with myself. I thought it was for rich people who drove up prices in the Cotswolds. I never felt guilty about Owl Cottage; there was hardly a queue for it, with its tiny backyard and weekday traffic noise. We hoped that buying it would be the first stage of a permanent move to Norfolk. Getting into our car, the BMW and its less flashy successors, I would imagine this was the final journey and that we were traveling in convoy with the removal van: that we were leaving the southeast behind forever. When I played this game, I would smile and my shoulders would relax. But then we would grind to a halt, at the sight of some carnage or disaster on the M25, and I would have to acknowledge that it was just another short, fraught weekend trip, and that the change in our lives would have to be earned.

For a time, we would visit every two or three weeks, our two cats traveling with us. Released, squalling, from their cage, they would race through the rooms, bellowing, feet thundering on the wooden stairs, driving out the devils only cats can see. Exhausted, they would take to their basket, while we climbed the stairs to a room papered the pale yellow of weak sunshine: better people already, calmer, kinder. On Saturday morning we would make a leisurely circuit of the Market Place, shop to shop, talking to people, posting our parcels, filling my many prescriptions, buying meat for our freezer. In the afternoon we would drive up to Holt to see my parents, with a bag of scones or a cake, some flowers, a book or two; then on Sunday my parents would drive to Reepham, and we would have lunch at the King's Arms or eat something cold at home: Cromer crabs, strawberries, Stilton. Then it was time to pack the car and go. Routinely, as we left, there was a small ache behind my ribs. I only count the happy hours.

My mother was a tiny, chic woman with a shaggy bob of platinum-colored hair. She usually wore jeans and a mad-colored sweatshirt, but everything she wore looked designed and meant; all the time I'd known her, since first I'd been able to see her clearly, she'd had that knack. My stepfather was younger than she was, by a few years, but he had undergone a coronary bypass, and his brown, muscular body seemed wasted. "Frail" was not a word I would have associated with him, but I noticed how his favorite shirt, soft and faded, clung to his ribs, and his legs seemed to consist of his trousers with articulated sticks inside. Once a draftsman, he had taken up watercolors, trying to fix onto paper the troubling, shifting colors of the coast; earlier in life, he would not have been able to tolerate the ambiguities and tricks of the light. Passion had wasted him, and anger; no one had given him a helping hand, he had no money when money mattered, and he was chronically exasperated by the evasions and crookedness of the world. He was honest by temperament;

the honest, in this world, give one another a hard time. He was an engineer. He wrote a small, exact, engineer's hand, and his mind was subdued to a discipline, but inside his chest his heart would knock about, like a wasp in an inverted glass.

I had been six or seven when Jack had first entered my life. In all those years, we had never had a proper conversation. I felt that I had nothing to say that would interest him; I don't know what he felt. Neither of us could make small talk. For my part, it made me tense, as if there were hidden meanings in it, and for his part . . . for his part I don't know. My mother thought we didn't get on because we were too much alike, but I preferred the obvious explanation, that we didn't get on because we were completely different.

Now, this situation began to change. Since his heart surgery, Jack had shown a more open and flexible personality than ever in his life. He had become more patient, more equable, less taciturn: and so I, in his presence, had become less guarded, more grown-up, more talkative. I found that I could entertain him with stories of the writers' committees I sat on in London; he had been a man who sat on committees, before his enforced retirement, and we agreed that whatever they were for ostensibly, all committees behaved alike, and could probably be trusted to transact one another's business. On that last afternoon, a bright fresh day toward the end of March, I hung back as we crossed the Market Place, so that my husband and my mother would walk ahead, and I could have a moment to tell him some small thing that only he would like. I thought, I have never done that before: never hung back, never waited for him.

He seemed tired when we got home after the meal. One of the cats, the striped one, used to lure him to play with her on the stairs. Until recently, he had loathed cats, denounced them like a Witchfinder General; he claimed to shrink at their touch.

But this tiny animal, with her own strange phobias, fright shivering behind her marzipan eyes, would invite him with an upraised paw to put out his hand for her to touch; and he would oblige her, held there by her mewing for ten minutes at a time, touching and retreating, pushed away and fetched back.

That last Sunday, when she took up her stance and invited him to begin, he stayed on the sofa, smiling at her and nodding. I thought, perhaps he is sickening for something: flu? But it was death he was sickening for, and it came suddenly, death the plunderer, uncouth and foulmouthed, kicking his way into their house on a night in April two or three hours before dawn. The doctor came and the ambulance crew, but death had arrived before them, his feet planted on the hearth rug, his filthy fingerprints on the pillowcase. They did their best, but they could have done their worst, for all it availed. When everything was signed and certified, my mother said, and the men had gone away, she washed his face. She sat by his body and because there was no one to talk to she sang in a low voice: "What's this dull town to me?/Robin's not near/He whom I wished to see/Wished for to hear . . ."

She sang this song to me when I was small: the tune is supersaturated with yearning, with longing for a lost love. About six o'clock she moved to the phone, but all her three children were sleeping soundly, and so she received only polite requests to leave the message that no one can ever leave. On and on we slept. "Where's all the joy and mirth/Made life a heaven on earth?/O they're all fled with thee/Robin Adare." About seven o'clock, at last, one of my brothers picked up the phone.

You come to this place, midlife. You don't know how you got here, but suddenly you're staring fifty in the face. When you turn and look back down the years, you glimpse the ghosts of other lives you might have led. All your houses are haunted by the person you might have been. The wraiths and phantoms creep under your carpets and between the warp and weft of your curtains, they lurk in wardrobes and lie flat under drawer liners. You think of the children you might have had but didn't. When the midwife says, "It's a boy," where does the girl go? When you think you're pregnant, and you're not, what happens to that child that has already formed in your mind? You keep it filed in a drawer of your consciousness, like a short story that wouldn't work after the opening lines.

In the February of 2002, my godmother Maggie fell ill, and hospital visits took me back to my native village. After a short illness she died, at the age of almost ninety-five, and I returned again for her funeral. I had been back many times over the years, but on this occasion there was a particular route I had to take: down the winding road between the hedgerows and the stone wall, and up a wide unmade track which, when I was small, people called "the carriage drive." It leads uphill to the old school, now disused, then to the convent, where there are no nuns these days, then to the church. When I was a child this was my daily walk, once in the morning to school and once again to school after dinner—that meal which the south of England calls lunch. Retracing it as an adult, in my funeral black, I felt a sense of oppression, powerful and familiar. Just before the public road joins the carriage drive came a point where I was overwhelmed by fear and dismay. My eyes moved sideways, in dread, toward dank vegetation, tangled bracken: I wanted to say, stop here, let's go no farther. I remembered how when I was a child, I used to think I might bolt, make a run for it, scurry back to the (comparative) safety of home. The point where fear overcame me was the point of no turning back.

Each month, from the age of seven to my leaving at eleven, we walked in crocodile up the hill from the school to the church to go to confession and be forgiven for our sins. I would come out of church feeling, as you would expect, clean and light. This period of grace never lasted beyond the five minutes it took to get inside the school building. From about the age of four I had begun to believe I had done something wrong. Confession didn't touch some essential sin. There was something inside me that was beyond remedy and beyond redemption. The school's work was constant stricture, the systematic crushing of any spontaneity. It enforced rules that had never been articulated, and which changed as soon as you thought you had grasped them. I was conscious, from the first day in the first class, of the need to resist what I found there. When I met my fellow children and heard their yodeling cry—"Good mo-or-orning, Missus Simpson," I thought I had come among lunatics; and the teachers, malign and stupid, seemed to me like the lunatics' keepers. I knew you must not give in to them. You must not answer questions which evidently had no answer, or which were asked by the keepers simply to amuse themselves and pass the time. You must not accept that things were beyond your understanding because they told you they were; you must go on trying to understand them. A state of inner struggle began. It took a huge expenditure of energy to keep your own thoughts intact. But if you did not make this effort you would be wiped out.

Before I went to school there was a time when I was happy, and I want to write down what I remember about that time. The story of my own childhood is a complicated sentence that I am always trying to finish, to finish and put behind me. It resists finishing, and partly this is because words are not enough; my early world was synesthetic, and I am haunted by the ghosts of my own sense impressions, which reemerge when I try to write, and shiver between the lines.

We are taught to be chary of early memories. Sometimes psychologists fake photographs in which a picture of their subject, in his or her childhood, appears in an unfamiliar setting, in places or with people whom in real life they have never seen. The subjects are amazed at first but then—in proportion to their anxiety to please—they oblige by producing a "memory" to cover the experience that they have never actually had. I don't know what this shows, except that some psychologists have persuasive personalities, that some subjects are imaginative, and that we are all told to trust the evidence of our senses, and we do it: we trust the objective fact of the photograph, not our subjective bewilderment. It's a trick, it isn't science; it's about our present, not about our past. Though my early memories are patchy, I think they are not, or not entirely, a confabulation, and I believe this because of their overwhelming sensory power; they come complete, not like the groping, generalized formulations of the subjects fooled by the photograph. As I say, "I tasted," I taste, and as I say, "I heard," I hear: I am not talking about a Proustian moment, but a Proustian cine-film. Anyone can run these ancient newsreels, with a bit of preparation, a bit of practice; maybe it comes easier to writers than to many people, but I wouldn't be sure about that. I wouldn't agree either that it doesn't matter what you remember, but only what you think you remember. I have an investment in accuracy; I would never say, "It doesn't matter, it's history now." I know, on the other hand, that a small child has a strange sense of time, where a year seems a decade, and everyone over the age of ten seems grown-up and of an equal age; so although I feel sure of what happened, I am less sure of the sequence and the dateline. I know, too, that once a family has acquired a habit of secrecy, memories begin to distort, because its members con-fabulate to cover the gaps in the facts; you have to make some sort of sense of what's going on around you, so you cobble together a narrative as best you can. You add to it, and reason about it, and the distortions breed distortions.

Still, I think people can remember: a face, a perfume: one true thing or two. Doctors used to say babies didn't feel pain; we know they were wrong. We are born with our sensibilities; perhaps we are conceived that way. Part of our difficulty in trusting ourselves is that in talking of memory we are inclined to use geological metaphors. We talk about buried parts of our past and assume the most distant in time are the hardest to reach: that one has to prospect for them with the help of a hyp-notist or psychotherapist. I don't think memory is like that: rather that it is like Saint Augustine's "spreading limitless room." Or a great plain, a steppe, where all the memories are laid side by side, at the same depth, like seeds under the soil.

There is a color of paint that doesn't seem to exist anymore, that was a characteristic pigment of my childhood. It is a faded, rain-drenched crimson, like stale and drying blood. You saw it on paneled front doors, and on the frames of sash windows, on mill gates and on those high doorways that led to the ginnels between shops and gave access to their yards. You can still see it, on the more soot-stained and dilapidated old buildings, where the sandblaster hasn't yet been in to turn the black stone to honey: you can detect a trace of it, a scrape. The restorers of great houses use paint scrapes to identify the original color scheme of old salons, drawing rooms, and staircase halls. I use this paint scrape—oxblood, let's call it—to refurbish the rooms of my childhood: which were otherwise dark green, and cream, and more lately a cloudy yellow, which hung about at shoulder height, like the aftermath of a fire.

Now Geoffrey Don't Torment Her

Two of my relatives have died by fire. One was my father's mother, whose name was Alice.

Alice was a widow. She was preparing to marry again, but a short while before the ceremony she saw her dead husband in the street. She took this as a sign to call it off.

A house fire killed her before I was born, even before my father married my mother. I've never seen her picture. She's gone.

The other victim of fire was from my mother's family. She was a little girl called Olive, who was burned to death when her nightdress caught alight. I know her because a photograph of her is set into a brooch. It is oval, which is the shape of melancholy, nostalgia, and lost romance. It shows a childlike smudge, unformed, without expression. On the other side of the brooch is George Foster, my maternal grandfather. He is a young soldier, grave, handsome, intent. If you wear the brooch, he is the natural choice to turn outward. No one, I guess, has ever put Olive on display. She gazes backward forever, blurred eyes on someone's breastbone; looking inside the body, like a child who has never left the womb.

I was born in 1952 and grew up in a village called Hadfield, which lies on the edge of moorland at the tip of the county of Derbyshire. It is close to the boundary of two other northern counties, Lancashire and Yorkshire, with which it shares rough terrain and a habit of deliberate speech. Less than two miles away is the border with Cheshire, a part of England which is usually seen as gentle, pastoral, and affluent. When my mother was a girl, she and her friends used to go down to the bridge that marked the border and throw stones at any coddled Cheshire children who crossed their line of sight.

England is a tiny country, and jealous of her demarcations. If you looked at a map in an unwary manner, you might place Derbyshire in the Midlands, and it is true that the south of the county has a sad Midlands character. But the area where I grew up is on the fringes of the Peak District, a place of complex geology and inventive forms of human deprivation, of inhospitable uplands and steep-sided valleys. Tiny fields, bordered by drystone walls, lie like a worn blanket on a pauper: sharp angles of limestone protrude like bony spurs through a token covering of green. On high ground, in the deep winters of my early life, snow lasted till April. At the fringes of the Peak, where limestone gives way to sandstone, icy streams tumble over brown boulders. There are miles of moorland, flat, featureless, sodden—trackless, or traversed by ancient, faded bridleways.

The moors are dangerous places, even for an experienced walker. If bad weather blows up—it can happen within minutes—you must be prepared to forget the evidence of your senses, and navigate by compass. The urbanite, tempted out by a sunny day, might think the going easy—until the sky seems to fall and enwrap his woolly hat, and a swirl of cold mist disorientates him and gets him walking in circles. People have died on the moors, people have been buried there. Britain's most notorious child-killers hid their victims in this terrain, and at least one of the bodies has never been found, despite the efforts of the woman who'd helped carry it there. You'd think that if you buried a murdered child, details of the scene would strike you, would you not? But here the details are too banal; the same country, seen from the riband of road, unscrolls and unscrolls, wet, dark, unrepentant, its ditches and verges jostled by the ghostly forms of Pennine sheep.

Two cities border on this space—Sheffield and Manchester. The village where I was born had grown up on its edge, nearer to Manchester. It is conventional to say that a village "nestles" in a valley; Hadfield squatted, like a fossil toad. The word "village" in itself invites indulgence: "an English village." Thatched cottages? Roses around the door? Community, closeness? Hadfield was a community; it was close. Every person oversaw the affairs of the next; and sniggered about them. Thatch would have been carried off by the wind. Roses were an ornament for more temperate climes. I had seen them in plastic, paper, fabric, and wax, but I was eleven before I studied and handled a rose that was growing, and my reaction to it was to render it lifeless again, a severed specimen, slowly delineating it with a nib pen and sepia ink.

There were flowers in the village, it's true. Dahlias bloomed effortfully in the park we called Bankswood, which soon ran out into wild country, as if it had given up the pose of civilization. There were few trees, little by way of shrubs or bushy cover, no places for birds to hide or nest. Urban birds thrived; a gangster band of pigeons swaggered down Bankbottom, the street where I was born. Or—I'd like to be precise—the street where I arrived home from hospital in the arms of my mother, Margaret Mary, a petite woman who could draw, sing, dance, arrange flowers, play the piano, and recite poems, a woman who—if she hadn't been a millworker—wouldn't have been out of place in a Jane Austen novel: and who now found herself unhappily married, and trapped. There was no divorce for Catholics. You could get an annulment, or run away. Nonconsummation was a usual ground for annulment; not easy to plead if you have a baby in your arms. Running away, with that burden, isn't an option either. She had to make the best of it, carrying her child upstairs to the front bedroom of her parents' house, which they had vacated for herself and her husband and her new daughter: squeezing up, as grandparents did in those days, to fit themselves into the smaller space of the freezing bedroom at the back of the house.

Much later, when I had a new, Protestant father, when my family made itself over and moved to Cheshire, I learned to name garden birds from a pocket manual with monochrome illustrations; I soon got good at magpies. A few years ago I bought myself a book called *The Easy Way to Tree Recognition,* admirably straightforward and systematic. The foreword is soothing: "In some ways, trees are easier to identify than birds. First and foremost, they never fly away." If you've got a tree, I say to myself, you can always put your hand on it, it won't flit or slip away. When you're somewhere else you can remember it, root and branch, as you can remember your life when it first put out its leaves. But is it simple or compound, and does it grow with a single stem? Are the leaves aromatic, are they hairy, heart-shaped, or toothed? "Does it have needles? How long are they? Do those needles have sharp tips?"

Hadfield squatted, so: sluiced by rain, battered by the four winds. Its streets were steep, its small houses gray and stony.

Textiles were its livelihood, but the industry was failing by the time I was born, and workers were gravitating to mills elsewhere, or to the factory which—like a factory in some grim period comedy—produced tinned meat and pickles. In the years after the Second World War, you might say grayness was a British condition, and it had not dispersed by 1952. As I grew up, and especially after I was eleven, my immediate family grew into a comparative prosperity: or at least, into a fraught, edgy imitation of it. But my mother often told me (claiming me for the war generation), "When you were born, you were given a number; you were issued a ration book." The times were meager, pared to the bone; in Hadfield, the wretched weather encouraged a grim view of life. Even the most svelte woman, stumping cobbled streets in the Hadfield winters, looked like one of those babushkas snapped in monochrome in a Moscow townscape: figure waddling and shapeless, eyes screwed up against the wind. The springs were late, the summers drenching and short; soon it was time to get out your wadding and your padding again, and face up to the skin-flaying attrition of the months from October to April.

The Cheshire town where we moved when I was eleven was barely a twenty minutes' drive away. Yet spring arrived there six weeks earlier, announced by the blossoming of ornamental cherry trees, by the cheerful whistling of the neighborhood's men as they turned back their shirt cuffs over winter wrists and carried cans of oil out to their garden sheds; by the sound of lawn mowers clearing their throats, trying an experimental cough before the season's pleasant work began. When summer rain fell, people said comfortably, the roses need it, don't they? Lovely for the lawns.

Possibly there was nothing to be done for Hadfield; as soon as I was able to reason about it I realized that leaving, preferably

soon, was the wisest course. I ask myself now, looking back—
if a ray of sun had shone through the deluge one spring day,
and a Hadfielder had by chance found the end of the rainbow,
what would that Hadfielder have done? Stared at the pot of
gold for an hour; kicked and turned it about; sniffed the ingots,
scratched at them with a fingernail; stamped them into the
soil and said—said what? Nothing, zero, zilch: in the dialect,
"nowt." Stomped into the pub scowling and said he'd found
this pot, eeeh, call that a pot, call that a rainbow, it's nobbut a
fraud. If the parable of the talents had been set in Hadfield, all
the talents would have been buried and no one would ever have
been able to find them again.

There was no overwhelming reason, except for the weather,
why the Hadfield people should have been so prosaic, distrust-
ful, and life-refusing. A good percentage of them were of Irish
descent like my own family, and had come in successive immigrant waves to serve the spinning machines and the looms. But
just as you must not indulge the word "village," you must not
indulge the word "Irish." The to-and-fro traffic with my family
in County Waterford seemed to have ended before I was born.
The best talker in my family was my grandfather, who was
English; it is possible of course that, as he was the man with the
steady job, he was the one who was allowed to hold the stage.
His income helped his wife Kitty's family when misfortune
struck: which seemed to be regular, like the strike of the clock.

When Kitty was a girl, she didn't go down to stone the
Cheshire children. At that date, tribal hatred had not resolved
into childish games, and the lines of demarcation were clear:
not the county boundary, but the religious divide. The Irish
fought the English every Saturday night, on a certain street
called Waterside; later when my mother would tell me this I'd
put my hands over my face, saying, "Yes, don't tell me again,"

protecting my own torn eyeballs and glassed scalp from the collective memory of damage. My mother thought the fighters were roaring boys, obeying some quaint, life-affirming custom, nation against nation. I thought they were tubercular wastrels propped up by drink, puncturing each other with shivs and costing their families the funeral money. I never imagined that I was part of their story. My role is behind the scenes, a sort of Scorcese continuity girl.

Someone has to pick up the bits of flying flesh, blot the blood, fake or not: and keep the narrative on track.

In Hadfield, you knew before you could walk which you were: us or them, Catholic or Protestant. It is true that by the 1950s we were less obviously, violently sectarian than our equivalents in the north of Ireland. Our religion didn't require us to throw petrol bombs, or for the men to kill one another on a weekend. But it did allow us—us Catholics, that is—to luxuriate in the knowledge that our neighbors were damned. They lived in the same cramped, cold row houses, without hot water or bathrooms, with the lavatories outdoors and a single fireplace in the downstairs room at the front. But we Catholics were getting mansions in heaven, with balmy breezes wafting, whereas they were getting their only warming in hell. They'd probably like to see a nice cheerful fire—until they were thrust into it.

A little girl—her name was Evelyn—was born a few doors away, six weeks before me. Our mothers had us playing together before we could walk, I suppose; Evelyn was part of my natural landscape, part of my own body, a thing that goes back beyond memory. I must have been three before I learned the word "friend," but then, when I learned what manner of thing she was, I registered her as separate, different. It was probably when we were three that we began to quarrel. Whenever we had an upset I would just check my temper and say, under my breath, "God help her, she's a Protestant, she doesn't know any better."

Evelyn was smart, slick, and sweet. She had limp dark hair, pinned away from her face by a slide made of plastic tortoiseshell; she had small eyes, slow to travel, their light kindled only by her constant and justified irritation with me. If there was a problem, she'd pull rank and scold, "I'm older than you!" It was true, and I never gave her a row about it, though I thought a birthday at the end of May was a barbarous thing; birthdays should be in July, like mine, when you had a half-chance of good weather. Evelyn grew angry when I criticized her birthday, but her smacks were small and theatrical and painless, administered with a flapping upraised palm; she was a girl, and did sly girly things like pinching. Two little creepers, eavesdroppers, we listened to everything adults said, took on their concerns, and turned them into games. We played Operation, which was about major surgery—a surprisingly bloodless, philosophical game, which involved no exposure of skin or body parts. We played School, which was far more violent; I never went down to Evelyn's end of the yard unless I was armed, so I made a tetchy teacher, likely to whip out a pistol or draw my sword if there was any disruption to the lesson. We played Wedding; monotonously, week after week, we married each other.

Evelyn collected postcards of ballerinas: frozen-faced women in black-and-white poses, a leg held stiffly in the air. One of them was called "Doreen Wells"—a name that seemed to me like a plunge into some dark, unfathomed Protestant pool. So that I had something to show Evelyn, my grandmother gave me the tiny cards that came out of tea packets: "Wildflowers." There were fifty-eight in the series. "We'll see if we can get them all," my grandad said. I didn't read the flowers' names, just their number; I pasted the cards against my face, and smelled the tea that had been breathed in by the paper.

Evelyn, when shown a tea card, simply drooped her wrists and worked her fingers disdainfully, as if she were shedding soiled kidskin gloves. "I'm quite artistic," she said, sighing, putting her head on one side; we had been watching television, in its infant form, and that is the kind of thing characters said. "Oh are you," I said. I was embarrassed to reveal that I didn't know what she meant. She was always catching me out in that way. But now I said, "Evelyn, do you know how to machine-gun? I have the complete instructions, and also how to go on if, God forbid, the mechanism should jam."

"Share and share alike," said Evelyn's mum, beaming down on us, rustling a brown paper bag from the greengrocer. "Share and share alike," Evelyn chirped, producing—how?—from the baggy sleeve of her cardigan a blunt fruit knife. With its useless blade and with her fingers she shredded and minced the fat plums her mother had given us. "We are not," she said, "each to have our own individual plums. We are sharing them."

I watched my fruit being mangled. Too communitarian, in my view: the fingers were too Protestant, mincy, thin. Small children taste each other's flesh, and I thought Evelyn's finger-tips—which I had sucked as often as I had sucked my own—had become alien as we grew. I never tried to convert her. I didn't think it could be done. You were just born that way. It was sad for her.

I can't make sense of childhood, I can only report it as it felt, minute by minute. I don't understand the terrain anymore, but I can walk it or trace it on a map. If you moved west out of

Hadfield, you moved into the milltown conurbations of Manchester, themselves saturated with immigrant Catholics. The railway would take you in less than forty-five minutes to the town itself, with its great soot-blackened university and Victorian hospitals, its trodden pavements slick with rain and the oily soles of shoes, its great bomb-sites and demolition areas, its fast, troubled urban pulse. But from any hillside in Hadfield, when you raised your eyes to the east you saw the moors, the hills, the infinite, opening space of danger, loss, the perpetual uncertainty of low dank cloud. It seemed to be a landscape in which theology and geography had got inextricably mixed. There was a topographical feature, ill understood by me, which was visible (or might have been, but for the mist and rain) from Hadfield's streets: people gestured into the murk, and mentioned "the Devil's Elbow." The road out over the moors was called the Snake; it appears on maps as the A57, the Snake Pass, Glossop to Sheffield. All this seemed acceptable to me, part of the unacknowledged strangeness of life; until I grew up and went away. First I had to learn to walk, to make a line, a confident line, a path of my own through my family, stumbling house to house: I am two years old.

This is the first thing I remember. I am sitting up in my pram. We are outside, in the park called Bankswood. My mother walks backward. I hold out my arms because I don't want her to go. She says she's only going to take my picture. I don't understand why she goes backward, back and aslant, tacking to one side. The trees overhead make a noise of urgent conversation, too quick to catch; the leaves part, the sky moves, the sun peers down at me. Away and away she goes, till she comes to a halt. She raises her arm and partly hides her face. The sky and trees rush over my head. I feel dizzied. The entire world is sound, movement. She moves toward me, speaking. The memory ends.

This memory exists now in black-and-white, because when I was older I saw Bankswood pictures: this photograph or similar ones, perhaps taken that day, perhaps weeks earlier, or weeks later. In the 1950s photographs often didn't come out at all, or were so fuzzy that they were thrown away. What remains as a memory, though the color has bled away, is the fast scudding of clouds and the rush of sound over my head, the wind in the trees: as if the waters of life have begun to flow.

Many years later, when there was a suspicion about my heart, I was sent to hospital for a test called an echocardiogram. A woman rolled me with a big roller. I heard the same sound, the vast, pulsing, universal roar: my own blood in my own veins. But for a time I didn't know whether that sound came from inside me, or from the depth of the machines by my bed.

I am learning, always learning. To take someone's picture, you move away from them. When you have finished, you move back.

The results of the test, I should say, were satisfactory. My heart was no bigger than one would expect.

I learn to walk in the house, but don't remember that. Outside the house, you turn left: I don't know it's left. Moving toward the next-door house: from my grandmother (56 Bankbottom Hadfield Near Manchester) to her elder sister, at no. 58. Embedded in the stonework on the left of my grandmother's door is a rusty iron ring. I always slip my finger into it, though I should not. Grandad says it is where they tied the monkey up, but I don't think they really ever had one ; all the same, he lurks in my mind, a small gray monkey with piteous eyes and a long active tail.

I have taken my finger from the ring, and tasted it for metal. I am looking down at the paving stones beneath the window. I have to pass the length of that window before I arrive at no. 58. I keep my eyes on the narrow stones which, placed edge to edge, form a curb. One, two, and the third is a raised, blueish stone, the color of a bruise, and on this stone, perhaps because it is the color of a bruise, I will fall and howl. Because I know I always, always cannot get past; and because howl is my stage of life, it is indulged in me. This goes on, till one day the consciousness of self-fulfilling prophecy enters my head. I decide I will not fall; I will not fall, and see what happens. I negotiate the bruise stone. It is the first time. Only once is needed. Now I can walk outside the house. I jump into the arms of my grandfather, George Foster, and I know I have nothing to fear.

At no. 58 the top of my head comes to the outermost curve of my great-aunt, Annie Connor. Her shape is like the full moon, her smile is beaming; the outer rim of her is covered by her pinny, woven with tiny flowers. It is soft from washing; her hands are hard and chapped; it is barely ten o'clock, and she is getting the cabbage on. "Hello, Our Ilary," she says; my family have named me aspirationally, but aspiration doesn't stretch to the "H." Rather embarrassed for her, that she hasn't spotted who I am, I slip her my name of the day. I claim I'm an Indian brave. I claim I'm Sir Lancelot. I claim I'm the parish priest and she doesn't quibble. I give her a blessing; she says, thank you, Father.

My head comes above the keyboard of the black piano. When you press a key the sound is bronchial, damaged; the piano at no. 56 has a more mellow note. I know how to find middle C because on the piano at no. 56 this key has a brown stain on the ivory, and a frill chipped out of it, as if some tiny animal has nibbled it. I am fond of the pianos, their two different voices and smells: the deep, disdainful, private aroma of their wood.

Nobody has told me yet that I am disastrously unmusical and had better leave the pianos alone. If someone will play I will stand at the side with my fingers on the wood and feel the resonance, the piano breathing and purring like a cat. I do not know a cat. Tibby is Mrs. Clayton's cat. He lives at no. 60, and flees along the wall. I do not know him. He is a Protestant cat. George Clayton is the first in the yard to rise in the morning, winter and summer long before dawn, treading from his house to the lavatory. I see him in the afternoon, coming home in broad day: a bulky figure in blue overalls, with a bulky blinkered head. One day he dies. Mrs. Clayton, people say, is "taken to Macclesfield": that is to say, she is mad. When she returns, the cat Tibby still flees along the wall. Instead of George, Mrs. Clayton gets a blunt-headed dog called Shula. The dog's kennel name, she tells me, is Shula Ballerina. It snaps and snarls and hurtles about the backyard. This does not prevent her going mad again.

In no. 58, Annie Connor starts a game. You go into a corner of the room. She into another. You both shout, very loud:

> *The wind blows east,*
> *The wind blows west,*
> *The wind blows o'er yon cuckoo's nest.*
> *Where is he*
> *That has to go*
> *Over yonder fields?*
> *Hi Ho!*

Then you just run about the room, screaming. So does she.

Two things not to believe: the monkey. People who say, "I have eyes in the back of my head."

I sit on the stairs, which are steep, boxlike, dark. I think I am going to die. I have breathed in a housefly, I think I have. The fly was in the room and my mouth open because I was putting into it a sweet. Then the fly was nowhere to be seen. It manifests now as a tickling and scraping on the inside of my throat, the side of my throat that's nearest to the kitchen wall. I sit with my head down and my arms on my knees. Flies are universally condemned and said to be laden with filth, crawling with germs, therefore what more sure way to die than swallow or inhale one? There is another possibility, which I turn and examine in my brain: perhaps the tickling in my throat is the sweet itself, which is a green sweet from a box of assorted candy called Weekend. Probably I shouldn't have eaten this one, but a jelly kind or fudge, more suitable to a child, and if I had hesitated and said I want that marzipan someone would have said, "That's bad for you," but now I'm on the stairs not knowing whether it's green sweet or fly. The fear of death stirs slowly within my chest cavity, like a stewpot lazily bubbling. I feel sorrow; I am going to miss seeing my grandparents and everyone else I know. I wonder whether I should mention the fact that I am dying, either from a fly or a green sweet. I decide to keep it to myself, as there won't be anything anyone can do. It will be kinder for them if they don't know; but I feel lonely, here on the stairs with my future shortening. I curse the moment I opened my mouth and let the fly in. There is a rasping, tickling sensation deep in my throat, which I think is the fly rubbing its hands together. I begin to wonder how long it will take to die. . . .

After a while I am walking about in the room again. My resolve to die completely alone has faltered. I suppose it will take an hour or so, or I might live till evening. My head is still hanging. What's the matter? I am asked. I don't feel I can say. My original intention was not to raise the alarm; also, I feel there is shame in such a death. I would rather just fall over, and that would be an end of it. I feel queasy now. Something is tugging at my attention. Perhaps it is a sense of absurdity. The dry rasping in my throat persists, but now I don't know if it is the original obstruction lodged there, or the memory of it, the imprint, which is not going to fade from my breathing flesh. For many years the word "marzipan" affects me with its deathly hiss, the buzz in its syllables, a sepulchral fizz.

My grandad goes on to the Red Lamp to take a gill. He puts on his checked sports coat and I shout, "Grandad is wearing his beer jacket." He puts on his suede shoes and I shout, "Grandad has put on his beer shoes." He takes up the pitcher from the kitchen shelf and I shout, "Grandad is taking his beer jug." However mild his habits, however temperate, I can't be stopped from chronicling his deeds.

The likes of a woman wouldn't go in the Red Lamp.

My grandfather knows about English things such as Robin Hood and Harvest Festival; I sit on his knee as he hums "All Things Bright and Beautiful." My grandmother says, "George, teaching that child Protestant hymns!" I dip my finger in his beer to taste it. For high days I have a thimble-sized glass to drink port. My grandmother says, "George, teaching that child to drink!" Slowly, slowly, we are pulling away from hearth and home and into the real world. My grandfather is a railway man and has been to Palestine, though not on the train. The spellings he teaches me include trick far-off towns such as Worcester and Gloucester: I cannot write, but no matter. As a grandfather, he knows the wherefores of cotton production, not just the facts of working in the mill. He knows about the American slaves and the Confederacy; also of a giant, name of Gazonka, who lives on a hill outside Glossop. Grandad has ancestors, unlike us Irish people, who don't know our correct birthdays even. One of his ancestors suppressed a riot by laying low a man called Murphy, a thug at the head of a mob who was wielding a wire whip. For this feat, his ancestor was rewarded with the post of sanitary inspector.

From Liverpool he brings jelly animals and a strange kind of balloon with faces and ears, and cardboard feet you can tie on it, to make it stand up. As no one can tell me the name for this item in God's creation, I name it "Fluke." If you don't know a word for something, you can just ask me to supply one, but I can't blow up a balloon; I have not breath. When he's not on his shift, Grandad's always at home, he's always in his parish. My grandmother's brothers come from Hollingsworth and places even farther. They give the impression, to me, of wandering the roads. They turn up unexpectedly; this is the time before telephones, or before anyone went anywhere, to be out when their relatives called. The brothers are indistinguishable elders in many woolen layers, who suck humbugs with loud slurps and sit on hard chairs with their caps still on: on hard chairs set each end of the sideboard, symmetrical, at the back of the room: as if an opera were about to burst out in front of the fireplace. My grandmother serves them a plate of ham and some Cheshire cheese. They cough long and wetly into their balled-up handkerchiefs, and even when they are not crying, their eyes seep.

When my grandmother wants her sister, she bangs on the wall. In other houses ghosts bang but here it's only Annie Connor, banging back.

The household at 56 Bankbottom lives in cooperation with the household at no. 58. Here lives, besides Annie Connor, her daughter, Maggie, who is my godmother and a widow, who has a brown raincoat and a checked woolen scarf. She does errands for people and is at their beck and call. Here lives Beryl, Maggie's daughter, my heroine: a schoolgirl, dimpled and saucy. There is only one doll for which I ever care, and that one, in tribute to her, is called Beryl. She is a doll made of grubby green satin, with satin stumps for hands and feet, features inked onto a round of calico for her face, and her pointed head of grubby green satin also.

My grandfather has to be knight and commander to all these women. His possessions are a billy can, a notebook and pencil, his guard's hat, and his guard's lamp. It is my ambition to be a railway guard.

In the desert my grandfather rode a camel. He commanded it with certain words in Egyptian, known only to camels, now imparted to me.

I am three. I sit on my grandmother's knee eating sponge cake warm from the oven. The cake is pale yellow and so high that I don't know whether to bite the bottom or the top; from deep experience I understand their different textures and tastes. We are by the fireplace, but the fire is not lit. Sun is shining. Outside the window people pass on the pavement. The back door stands open.

From hooks below the shelf hang two jugs, each of which holds one pint (though not at this moment). One is a rich cream and the other is the palest pink. They curve fatly from their lips, and the light gilds the curve: one a milk skin, one a shell. The table has fat, green, complicated legs. I go under the table to run my fingertip over their convolutions. The table's top is scrubbed white wood. The knots are like glass. I am comforted to think that next door at no. 58, our dog, Rex, is under the table, just like me. Peas flick from their pods into a white enamel colander, which has a rim of navy blue. The scent of inner peapod rises around me. I count the peas. I tug the embryonic peas from the stalk, and count them as half, or quarter. My grandmother makes strawberry pie. A question people pose is, "How many beans make five?"

I used to be Irish but I'm not sure now. My grandmother was born on Valentine's Day, or so she always believed; my mother says that Annie Connor, being the eldest, gave out to her brothers and sisters the birthdays she thought they would like. Now someone has produced an official paper, and Grandma's birthday's got altered to the first of March. Everyone laughs at her. She laughs too, but she's not happy to change. They say she used to be our Valentine, but now she's a Mad March Hare. Her name is Kitty, sometimes Kate; before she married she was called O'Shea. Her mother—before she married—was called Catherine Ryan. She was a small illiterate lady with an upright walk. An old person who remembers her has told my mother, "While you are alive and walking, Catherine Ryan will be alive." Or words to that effect.

Much later, when I'm in my teens, my godmother lets it slip that Catherine Ryan was fond of a drink. We have to revise our mental picture of this famous walk of hers, and my mother is no longer so pleased about the comparison. I defend my great-grandmother, saying that I'm not surprised if she took a drink: surely she was like the old woman who lived in a shoe, she had so many children that she didn't know what to do? Ten, eleven, twelve? I'm always losing count; there's Paddy and Martin and Daniel and Joe, there's John and Joanna and Mick. And why did her husband leave her, alone with all those babies? My mother says, it wasn't his fault; he would have come back to her, Patrick Ryan, if only she had made it possible. My mother is usually on the side of men; I'm, usually, not. Grandma says: one thing about my mammy, anyway, she may have taken a drink but she never smoked a pipe. And oh, she knew how to cook cabbage!

My mother says: "Monday's child is fair of face, Tuesday's child is full of grace, Wednesday's child is full of woe, Thursday's child has far to go, Friday's child works hard for a living, Saturday's child is loving and giving, but the child that is born on the Sabbath day, is blithe and bonny, good and gay."

I have various thoughts about this. I think my mother must be Monday's child. I know I am born on Sunday but it would be complacent to dwell on it. Besides, I think any parent would prefer Saturday's child. I ask, which day is my daddy? She doesn't miss a beat. I think it must be Thursday, she says, because he has to go into town every day.

My father, Henry, is tall and thin, with a tweed sports jacket. His black hair is slicked back with a patent solution. He wears spectacles and looks very intelligent, in my opinion. He brings home the *Manchester Evening News*.

When he comes in from work he carries on his coat the complex city smell of smog, ink, tobacco. He has a traveling chess set, its leather cover worn, which folds up and slides into a pocket. The chessmen, red and white, fit into the boards by tiny pegs. I can play with them, but not the proper game. I am not old enough, wait till I am seven. (He might as well say, wait till you're forty-five, for all that seven means to me.) With his good pen, Henry completes the crossword puzzle in the paper. I sit on his knee while this occurs. To help him, I hold his pen, and click the ballpoint in and out, so it won't go effete and lazy between clues. I like to get close to people who are thinking, to glue myself to the warm, buzzy, sticky field of their concentration. Henry reads the racing page. It is horses who race. To aid him, I imagine the horses. He says their names. I picture them strenuously.

With my mother and my father Henry I go on the green electric train, the same color as my raincoat; this coat I have picked specially, as blending in with the electric train; it has an industrial smell of rubber. When we step into the train, with its wide automatic doors, I take the hands of my mother and father and ensure that we all step in together, leading off with the same foot. I am afraid someone will get left behind, and I believe that once the doors have swooped closed you can't open them again. Suppose one person stepped on first, and the doors closed, and that person was on the train alone, sent ahead: worst of all, suppose that person should be me?

We go to Manchester, to Mrs. Ward, my father's grandmother. (Alice, his mother, has gone up in the fire.) My great-grandfather is still alive and sitting in the back room by the range, but nobody seems to take much notice of him. He has white hair and a black suit and a watch chain across his meager belly; I designate him the trade of watchmaker. My Manchester great-grandmother is diminutive even by my standards, with a skull the size of an orange. She takes me upstairs and opens a chest, out of which she takes scraps of shiny, silky fabric. These are to dress my dolls, she explains. I am too polite to say I don't dress dolls, or sew with stitches.

When my mother sees the scraps, she assumes a look of scorn. Scorn is a beautiful word. He curls his bearded lip in scorn. Bastion is a beautiful word, as are citadel, vaunt, and joust. Anyone who hesitates near me, these days, has to read me a chapter of *King Arthur and the Knights of the Round Table.* I am considering adding knight errant to the profession of railway guard. Knight errant means "knight wanderer," but I also think it means "knight who has made a mistake." Mistakes are made all the time; it is a human thing, in a knight, to slip up once in a while.

I am waiting to change into a boy. When I am four this will occur.

I suppose the trips to Manchester occupied a span of years; first the three of us went, then just myself and Henry. I had a dread of the streets and roofscapes, which were like a trap. I was used to looking up and seeing hills. The bay-windowed redbrick houses seemed to me squalid, though they were larger and better appointed than the stone-built millworkers' cottages in Hadfield. My cousin Geoffrey, a large boy, was told off to take me to the park. It was a gritty walk on the endless pavements, under the secondhand sky, and when you arrived there was only a rabbit of limited interest, twitching its nose through wire. I do not remember Geoffrey's face at all, only his huge legs in flapping flannel shorts, the blunt bony bulk of his knees. He was my adopted cousin, I was told; I wonder why, out of all the things that weren't explained, this one thing was explained to me. Back at the house Geoffrey would trap me between items of furniture, sticking out one of those huge legs to prevent me toddling the way I meant to go, then when I turned back barring me with an outstretched arm, so that I revolved about and about in a tearful muddle. He was teasing, he meant me no harm. I saw myself through his eyes, silly, frilly, too tiny to outwit him or hit him, baby fists clenched in exasperation. And this picture dismayed me, so far was it at odds with my own image of myself. In my own mind, I was already at least middle-aged. My judgment of Geoffrey was that only the accident of my small size concealed my great superiority to him in every way. And this made it doubly galling, that I was stuck in an alley between armchairs, and would be rotating there until somebody noticed and said, "Now Geoffrey don't torment her . . ."

Sitting up at the big table with a white cloth, we ate ham and tongue. The white plates were icy to the touch. Once I asked my mother, "Why do we always have ham and tongue?" She snapped, "Because you said you liked it." I am amazed; I don't expect my likes to have any sway in the world, and clearly, neither does she.

The journeys home I don't remember. I expect I was poleaxed with fatigue, what between Geoffrey and the rabbit and the watchmaker and the strain on my mother's face. I left us to herd onto the train any way we could.

"Ward" means watch, it can be a place of surveillance, it can be the name for a defensible segment within a castle: a place for sentinels.

I have a friend! It is Evelyn, a Protestant. I have to go down the yard to play with her; go on, Grandma says, smiling on the doorstep, and I turn my face around and say, why? She says, Evelyn, you know Evelyn, you want to play with Evelyn, don't you? She's your friend.

Oh, is she? I have some vague idea about the girl. I seem to think that before this we were carried like rival sultans to view each other, our retainers bearing us to the rendezvous in their arms; or bounced down Bankbottom in our big springing per-ambulators, to wave our woolly mittens at each other, and acknowledge each other with dips of our bonnets; like commanders from rival galleons bobbing on the sea.

But now I can go on on my own legs; Grandma lifts me over the step, and sets me down carefully, with my face pointing to Evelyn's house. My mother—who must, in her simplicity of heart, have intended no more breeding—had by this date sold my pram to another family. When I saw it in the street I dis-graced her by chasing it, bawling as if they had driven it away without authority. But she broke it to me that the pram would never come back; I nodded, and promised not to embarrass her again, or at least not in quite that way. For long distances, at this stage, I have a minor conveyance called a trolley, low-slung with wheels and a hood that folds back on itself like wrinkling tar; but generally I get about under pedestrian power, my fat legs goose-stepping in their green-and-white gingham, my feet in sandals slapping each paving stone as I pass, my sunsuit—for this is summer—hung about with my impedimenta: my small arms, my notebook and pencil for making scribble, my lamp or torch shining out into the broad daylight: my flopping white sunhat on my head. Two doors down lives my uncle Martin and his wife, Harriet; both are dead. I am told Harriet died before I was born; I do not think things can have happened before I was born, and I hope to defeat the notion by seeing Harriet emerge, wearing the large, petaled hat she sports in her photographs. From under the rim of my own hat I peep upward at their closed back door; and pass it. I totter down to see what, by way of heathen excitement, the Aldouses have got prepared.

Evelyn's mother is wrapped about and about in a big pinny. She is cheerful and talks in a Scottish way. My mother calls her Kath, which I think a melting name. She teaches me to say "Kirkcudbrightshire": which is where she comes from, as I come from no. 56. When she gives me my dinner she puts the salt already on it; Grandad has noticed that I don't take salt, but she can't know that. Her legs in thick dark stockings are the shape of big beer bottles, so when anyone says, "Stout," I think of Evelyn's mum.

Evelyn's house—the Aldouses' house—is darker than ours and has a more dumpling smell. Not being Catholics, they don't have a piano, but as they are at the end of the common yard, they have a more tidy and well-arranged plot, with flower beds. Outside our house my grandad has grubbed out a bed for nasturtiums, and trained them up a wall. He calls them storshions, and says you can pickle and eat the seeds, good in what they call a sallet, but I think, what a waste. My whole vision is filled with these pale leaves, these flowers. When I try to put names to their imperial colors, to the scarlet and striated amber, my chest seems dangerously to swell; I imagine them to be musical instruments, broadcasting stately and imperial melodies from their own hearts, because their shape is like that of gramophone horns, which I have seen in pictures. These flowers combine every virtue, the portentous groan of brass, the blackish sheen of crimson: to the eye, the crushable texture of velvet, but to the fingertip, the bruise of baby skin.

Evelyn's dad, Arthur, grows geraniums. Their flowers are scarlet dots, their stems are bent and nodular. When Arthur comes in from work in his bib and brace, his sleeves are rolled up above his elbows, and I see the inside of his arms, the sinews and knotty veins. I think his arms are the stems of plants, that he is not human, perhaps an ogre. When I hear him at the front door I run out of the back door and run home.

I am aware, as time passes, that adults talk about this, and that it makes them laugh. He who laughs last, I think darkly. Evelyn's father has sap, not blood. If they don't know he's dangerous, so much the worse for them. Fear is nothing to be ashamed of, nor is running away, when the retreat is tactical and the enemy is a green man.

I am four. Four already! Ivy Compton-Burnett describes a child with "an ambition to continue in his infancy," and I have that ambition. I am fat and happy. When I am asked if I would like to give up my cot for a sweet little bed, the answer is no. Every day I am busy: guarding, knight errantry, camel training. Why should I want to move on in life?

My grandfather lifts me up and sits me on his folded arms. We scan Albert Street, a cobbled road that runs at the end of our yard. Unsmiling, he nods his head across the street, to where there is a sturdy wall, higher than a man, topped with vast, flat flags, so broad an army could march on them. Its stones are black with soot, and it is a wall so sturdy, so formidable, that it appears it will stand forever. He says, without emphasis, almost casually, "Your great-grandfather built that wall." I feel his sturdy pride, I feel the strength of his arms. I think, we built everything!

At the back of the yard is a nursery school, a prefabricated building with a plaque on it, to say that it was opened by Lady Astor; I employ someone to read it out to me. My grandfather tells me the people from the nursery hang over the back wall, saying can't Ilary come to our school? But he says, he tells me, that he wants my company, that I am too useful about the place. Grandad and I have special food, at different times from other people. When he comes off his shift he eats alone, tripe, rabbit, distinctive food that is for men. Around noon each day I take a lamb chop, and a slice of bread and butter.

Winter: we go to the pantomime. We sit high up in a box, in the dark of the afternoon. I like the box better than Mother Goose. A man wearing ordinary man's clothes comes out onto the stage. He holds up his arms. He says to the audience, "I am Anthony Eden." The audience roars at him. I know he is not.

Two problems occur. First, the spaniel. From time to time a dog would trot down the steps to our yard, look about with its tail wagging, and then trot away again. It was a decrepit dog, aged and shapeless; I had been seeing it for a long time. It had a long sad face and was brown-and-white in patches. "When I was young," I said diffidently, "I used to think that dog was a cow." I was hoping to prompt the reply, "Well, actually, secretly, it is," but the reply I got was, "Don't be silly."

I knew it was a dog. But I couldn't help thinking that, in some way, and secretly, it was a cow. Deception seemed to be in the air. The true nature of things was frequently hidden. No one would say plainly what was what: not if they could help it.

Somehow, I got into trouble. I was supposed to have said that my friend Evelyn was a liar. She had complained to her mother, Kath, about it. The word "liar," I now learned, was a terrible word, prohibited, and one such as no child might say. Even if one adult were to say it to another, it would still be a cause of scandal.

Mrs. Aldous came down the yard to complain to my mother. She stood and looked stout. There were high words. My mother took me aside and spoke to me tactfully. She was trying to negotiate a formula that would suit all parties. She put it to me: "Is it possible that you said, 'Evelyn, you tell lies?'" I denied it. No such conversation had taken place. I was baffled. There were more high words, family to family. I stopped Kath as she was crossing the yard. I wanted to have this out. I put my hand up to detain her, and tugged at her pinny. "I didn't say it," I told her. She leaned over me, smiling, oozing Scots sweetness, her hands spread on her thighs: "Ahh, but lovie, you did."

The incident fizzled out somehow. I was left with a sense of injustice and bewilderment. My friend had lied about my having said she lied. Why? Must she always be believed, and me never? I knew I had not uttered the words complained of, because I was not concerned with whether she told lies. She was a steady and regular confabulator, but what could you expect of someone with a plant for a father? I could hardly say that in my defense. It seemed like one of those knots that gets harder to untie the more you try to pull it apart.

I sensed more trouble ahead. One of these days I had to go to school. My mother, who worked as the school secretary, had already brought a reading book home and tried to coax me toward it. I had taken it up secretly, and been knocked back by the "Introduction for Teachers." When my mother turned the pages and showed me the short, squat, words I would be required to master, I was simply not interested.

My grandad, when he was under arms, was an instructor in the Machine Gun Corps. It was he who would teach me all my martial arts. He could still recite the manual for the Vickers Gun, tripod-mounted, belt-fed, and I learned it from him, just as, when she was a child, my mother had learned it. I expect we thought it would be handy.

I spent time with my grandmother, time with her sister Annie. At no. 58 they sat by the fire on upright chairs, wooden and unforgiving; they were old, I thought, but sadly had no armchairs. They talked and talked, in an interweaving pattern of old and interesting words, and the refrain was, "Kitty, we were born too soon. Oh, Kitty, Kitty. I wish I were ten years younger." "Oh Annie, we were, and so do I." Annie Connor says she hopes she will never hate anyone, but the thing she could not fail to hate was a Black and Tan. And for people of the Orange persuasion she can't care. My grandmother simply doesn't speak on the topic. I think if a Black and Tan came to the door looking peckish, she would probably feel sorry for him and make him a strawberry pie.

At no. 56, only my grandfather occupied an armchair, his cigarette between his fingers, his brass ashtray balanced on the chair arm. Women didn't take their ease; when young, I thought, they ran about, and when old, they perched on upright chairs until they died, simply slumping to the linoleum, knocking their heads on the fireplace, and waiting to be carried away to the undertaker, Mr. Worsley, who buried Catholics. Maggie, Annie Connor's daughter, was neither old nor young. She never sat down. Neither did my mother, nor my cousin Beryl. My grandmother was so creased by anxiety that her face resembled a pleated skirt. Like her elder sister's, her hands were fat, with cracked and harsh palms, and I thought she had got these from washing clothes with Fairy Soap, from wiping the fireplace with Vim. Grandma was forever on hands and knees, mopping, towing a little flat black mat she called "me kneelin' mat." When someone came to the door, and she didn't know who it was, she would hide on the stairs. She never went out. Officially this was because of her bad leg but I knew there were other reasons and I was sorry for them: like a child, she was too shy to speak to strangers. When something made her laugh, tears sprang out of her eyes, and she swayed on her hard chair: swayed as much as her corsets allowed, and creaked. She and Annie Connor had the most terrible corsets, salmon-pink: like the Iron Maiden, from which their heads stuck out.

My mother would tell me, later, of her parents' narrow and unimaginative nature. My grandmother had become a mill-worker when she was twelve years old; my mother herself was put into the mill at fourteen. She was of diminutive size and delicate health; she was pretty and clever and talented. Her school, by some clerical error, had failed to enter her for the scholarship exam that would, her parents permitting, have sent her to grammar school. But it didn't matter, she said later, because they would not have permitted it. It would have been just as it was for her father, a generation earlier, for George Clement Foster pounding the cobbled streets of Glossop: circa 1905, he ran all the way home, shouting, "I've passed, I've passed." But there was no money for the uniform; anyway, it just wasn't what you did, go to the grammar school. You accepted your place in life. My mother would have liked to go to art school, but on Bankbottom nobody had heard of such a thing. She applied for a clerical job by competitive exam, but it went to a girl called Muriel; poor Muriel, she got all the questions wrong, my mother said, but you see her uncles had pull. Thwarted, unhappy, she stayed in the mill and earned, she said, a wage as good as a man's. The work was hard and took a painful toll on immature muscle and bone. It would be many years before the effects showed; but in those days, with energy to spare, she danced and sang through her evenings, in amateur shows and pantomimes. "Cinderella" was her favorite part. Her favorite scene: the Transformation. She asked herself, could she really be the child of her parents? Or some changeling princess, dropped into Bankbottom by accident?

For the whole of my childhood I worried about the glass slipper. It is such a treacherous object to wear: splintering, and cutting the curved, tender sole of the dancing foot. The writer Emily Prager once said that she had rewritten, as a child, the second half of the story; Cinderella gets to the ball and breaks her leg. My own feelings were similar; the whole situation was too precarious, you were too dependent on irresponsible agents like pumpkins and mice, and always there was midnight, approaching, tick-tock, the minutes shaving away, the minutes before you were reduced to ashes and rags. I was relieved, as an adult, when I learned that the slipper was not of verre, but of vair: which is to say, ermine. The prince and his agents were ranging the kingdom with a tiny female organ in hand—his ideal bride, represented by her pudendum. Never mind her face: he had not raised his eyes so far. All he knew was that the fit was tight.

Three, four, I am still four: I think I will be it forever. I sit on the back doorstep to have my picture taken. Fair hair gushes from under my bonnet. My clothes are a pair of brown corduroy trousers and a pink woolly cardigan with a zip; I call it a windjammer. I have another just the same but blue. I have a yellow knitted jacket, double breasted, that I call a Prince Charles coat. Summer comes and I have a crisp white dress with blackberries on, which shows my dimpled knees. I have a pink-and-blue frock my mother doesn't like so much, chosen by me because it's longer; people of six, I think, have longer skirts, and I am beginning to see that youth cannot last forever, and now hope to be taken for older than I am. The onset of boyhood has been postponed, so far. But patience is a virtue with me.

We go to the seaside, to Blackpool, to stay at Mrs. Scott's boardinghouse. Just the three of us: my mother, my father, myself. I insist that we stand before a mirror, all three. They are to pick me up and hold me between them, my fat arms across their shoulders, my hands gripping them tight. I call this picture "All Together"; I insist on its title. I know, now, that this tableau, this charade, must have caused them a dull, deep pain. We do it time and time again, I insist on it and I am good at insisting. As a knight I am used to arranging siege warfare, the investment of major fortresses, so the reluctance and distraction of a couple of parents isn't going to stop me pulling life into the shape I want it to be.

Standing on the pier at Blackpool, I look down at the inky waves swirling. Again, the noise of nature, deeply conversational, too quick to catch; again the rushing movement, blue, deep, and far below. I look up at my mother and father. They are standing close together, talking over my head. A thought comes to me, so swift and strange that it feels like the first thought that I have ever had. It strikes with piercing intensity, like a needle in the eye. The thought is this: that I stop them from being happy. I, me, and only me. That my father will throw me down on the rocks, down into the sea. That perhaps he will not do it, but some impulse in his heart thinks he ought. For what am I, but a disposable, replaceable child? And without me they would have a chance in life.

The next thing is that I am in bed with a fever raging. My lungs are full to bursting. The water boils, frets, spumes. I am limp in the power of the current that tugs beneath the waves.

To open my eyes I have to force off my eyelids the weight of water. I am trying to die and I am trying to live. I open my eyes and see my mother looking down at me. She is sitting swiveled toward me, her anxious face peering down. She has made a fence of Mrs. Scott's dining chairs, their backs to my bed, and behind this barrier she sits, watching me. Her wrists, crossed, rest on the backs of the chairs; her lady's hands droop. For a minute or two I swim up from under the water: clawing. I think, how beautiful she is: Monday's child. Her face frames a question. It is never spoken. My mother has brought her own bed linen, from home, and below my hot cheek, chafing it, is a butterfly: spreading luxuriant wings, embroidered on the pillowcase by my mother's own hand. I see it, recognize it, put out my hot fingers to fumble at its edges. If I am with this butterfly, I am not lost but found. But I can't stay. I am too hot, too sick. I feel myself taken by the current, tugged away.

I am changed now. Not in that fever but in one of the series, one of those that follow it, my weight of hair is cut off. What remains is like feathers, I think, like fluff. I lose my baby fat. For another twenty-five years I will be frail. In my late twenties I have a narrow rib cage, a tiny waist, and a child's twig-arms fuzzed with white-gold hair. At twenty-nine I am cast as a ghost in a play: as Noël Coward's Blithe Spirit, walking with noiseless slippered feet, a phantom of air and smoke. But then my life will change again, and I will find myself, like one of Candia McWilliam's characters, "barded with a suit of fat." I will be solid, set, grounded, grotesque: perpetually strange to myself, convoluted, mutated, and beyond the pale.

All of us can change. All of us can change for the better, at any point. I believe this, but what is certainly true is that we can be made foreign to ourselves, suddenly, by illness, accident, misadventure, or hormonal caprice. I am four, and my mother tells me this story about myself: that when I was born my hair was black and thick. At the age of five I mourn for it, weaving in my mind the ghost of a black plait that trails over my right shoulder. Once, I say to myself, I was a Red Indian. I get a feathered headdress and a tepee, bought for me in Manchester: so clear am I about my new requirements, about my antecedents. The tepee is erected in the middle of my grandmother's floor and in it I have a small chair and small table. People step around me. I take my meals in the tepee, and believe my hands are brown, as they wield the spoon. But already it feels like a game, whereas in some previous time, in another life, I believe I had a right to this kit. I know that there is no truth in this belief. But it has created in me a complex emotion; what I feel, for the first time, is nostalgia.

It is 1957. Davy Crockett is all the go. I get a fur hat with a tail. We sing a stupid song that says Davy, Davy Crockett, is king of the wild frontier. It makes me want to laugh but I'm not sure who the joke's on. We sing he killed a bear when he was only three. Somehow I doubt it. Even I didn't do that.

Where are the knights of the Round Table? In abeyance, while I get to grips with how the West was won. Now another thing occurs. I make a fuss! It is related to my role in life. When exactly do I become a boy?

My mother and father have been to Manchester, without me. We have brought you a present, they say, as they take off their coats. What is it? Well, it is a cottage set. It is taken out, extracted from a long cardboard box which has a cellophane window to show its contents. It is a doll's tea set, a teapot, milk jug, and sugar bowl made to look like rustic cottages, with little doors and windows: though only the teapot has a roof, a thatched one. I am puzzled at first—what is the use of it or where is the amusement to be derived? Then they say, we have bought your cousin Christopher a shooting range! A shooting range? I open my mouth and bawl. Shooting range!

Well! I can hear them saying. She did make a fuss! We had to give it her!

The shooting range consisted of a metal bar on a stand, which you placed on the carpet. On the bar swung four crude animal shapes made of molded plastic, painted in primary colors. I only remember the owl; perhaps it was the only one I recognized, or perhaps I knew that people don't shoot owls. You were supplied with a tiny rifle, which shot out a cork. You had to lie on your belly, very close, if you were going to hit the animals; you knew you had hit them if you made them swing on the bar. That was all there was to it. I found the thing tame. I had thought "a shooting range" would entail actual destruction. Slaughter.

Everyone is disappointed. Them, because they thought I was too mature for the shooting range; and it was true, I was. And me, because I can't get to grips with this cottage set at all. They must have bought it for someone else. Some ideal daughter that they don't have. It hangs about the house though; the teapot, unused, sits in the china cabinet, looking silly, but my mother keeps hair grips in the doll's cottage that is meant to be a sugar basin. Years pass. A dozen sets of crockery are smashed, but the cottage survives. The edges of its tiny windowpanes accrete a rim of grime. And grimly, night after night, my mother studs the grips into my hair, trying to impart a curl. In time my shorn hair grows again: gray-blond, straight, down to my waist and as flimsy as a veil. "The weight pulls the curl out," my mother protests. But the curl isn't ever there, nor is the weight.

I am only playing, inside the Indian's tepee, and I know it. I have lost the warrior's body I had before the fever. My bullet-like presence, my solidity, has vanished. Ambiguity has thinned my bones, made me light and washed me out, made me speechless and made me blond. I realize—and carry the dull knowledge inside me, heavy in my chest—that I am never going to be a boy now. I don't exactly know why. I sense that things have slid too far, from some ideal starting point.

Later, when I am six, I am given a black doll. My mother wants to bring me up to mother all races. The doll is huge, half as big as me. She cries "mama" when you rock her: if you bother. Her tiny lips are scarlet, and they are parted to show the tip of her scarlet tongue. Her hair is close-cropped wool. She wears a white frilly dress. I know that, if I tow her about, I will make it grubby; this is a peril I have no intention of entering into. I recognize the probable expense of the doll, and that—in some way—she belongs to my mother who has procured her. Her pottery forehead is hard against my lips.

My mother and father sit together in the front room of 56 Bankbottom. It is afternoon, summer, perhaps four o'clock; I am stupidly slow about telling the time. Certain hours bring their charged, unmistakable light, the low rays slanting through the glass. They are sitting with a chess board between them; not the traveling set, for no one is going anywhere today. Black men and white: neither makes a move. The house is quiet. Where are the others? I don't know. I am intimate with the chess pieces, the knight being still my favorite: his prancing curved neck, his flaring equine muzzle. The silence draws itself out, a long note in music; the light glitters with dust motes. No one moves, neither man nor woman; their hands are still, their eyes cast down. The pieces quiver, waiting to be touched: the black and the white, the smooth-skulled bishop, tall and powerful queen: the pawns, babyish and faceless. And so many of the latter: toddling across the board, so quickly nudged out of line and ventured, so easily picked off by snipers, and dropped back to coffined oblivion in the wooden box with its sliding lid. I understand the game, almost. The groove in the bishop's head fits the nail of my little finger, and the white pieces are of pale wood, grain swirling around their curves: the heads of the pawns, imagined beneath my fingertips, roll like shelled peas. Light, dust, silence; four o'clock.

A noise rips open the air. My parents raise their heads. It is a motorcycle, unsilenced, tearing open the afternoon, snarling down the street: 60 miles an hour. It rattles the windows; it is loud enough to wake babies, to frighten dogs. Then in an instant it has passed us, the noise fading to a snarl; changing and dying, in no time at all, to a long and melancholy drone, to a sigh. No one has spoken. But we have heard. Someone clears their throat: not me. They shift in their chairs. Their heads droop again. The racket, the roar, lasted for seconds, but the inner ear replays it and cannot help: winding away, with an afternote like vapor on the breeze, down the long and winding road.

I think, I shall remember this. I shall remember this forever; this dying note, the slanting light, their bent heads. It is a moment of pure self-consciousness, the foretaste of what is to come. I know, besides, that they are not looking at the chess board; they are looking, covertly, at each other's faces.

I went to school, taking my knights—small, gray, plastic knights, in a bag. They were for a rainy day. My mother said this would be all right.

One had simply never seen so many children. It took me a few days to establish their complete ignorance. Evelyn I had got trained, to a degree, but no one here understood anything of the arts of war. Giant Gazonka? They didn't know him. Machine gunning? They simply looked blank. Suppose a camel came in, and they had to command him? They went around with their mouths hanging open and their noses running, with silver trails from nostril to top lip: with their cardigans bagging and sagging, their toes coming out of their socks, their hair matted and their bleary eyes revolving anywhere but where they should look. When they came back after dinnertime, they stood in their places, beside their infant chairs, and gawped at the blackboard. Thereon was the chalked word "Writing." The children chorused, "Wri-i-i-ting." After a few days of this, I thought it would be a mercy if I varied the performance by clapping my hands and singing it, to a syncopated rhythm: wri-ting wri-tingg! Mrs. Simpson said, "Do you want me to hit you with this ruler?" I made no answer to this. Obviously I didn't, but I didn't either know why she proposed it.

I kept my bounce for a week or two, my cheerful preschool resilience; I was a small pale girl, post-Blackpool, but I had a head stuffed full of chivalric epigrams, and the self-confidence that comes from a thorough knowledge of horsemanship and swordplay. I knew, also, so many people who were old, so many people who were dead: I belonged to their company and lineage, not to this, and I began to want to rejoin them, without the interruptions now imposed. I couldn't read, but neither could any of the other children, and it was a wearisome uphill trail in the company of Dick and Dora, Dick and Dora's dog and cat, who were called Nip and Fluff, Dick and Dora's Mummy, and Dick and Dora's gar-den. Sometimes Dad-dy put in an appearance, and if my memory serves he was balding and tweedy. It was dull stuff, all of it, and as my head was already full of words, whole sagas which I knew by heart, I was not convinced that it was necessary. Before I was entrusted with paper I was given chalk and a slate, but the slate was so old and thick and shiny that the letters slipped off as I tried to chalk them. At the end of the morning I could only show letters up to D. Mrs. Simpson expressed surprise and disappointment. She didn't threaten violence. I was given plasticine to work the letters in. Instead of making them flat on the table I wanted to make them stand up, so by the time the bell rang I was, once again, only up to D. I was giving a fair impression of a child who was slow and stupid. I was both too old and too young for the place I had arrived at. My best days were behind me.

One of my difficulties was that I had not understood school was compulsory. I thought that you could just give it a try and that if you didn't like it you were free to revert to your former habits. To me, it was getting in the way of the vital assistance I gave my grandad, and wasting hours of my time every day. But then it was broken to me that you had to go; there was no option. Not to go, my mother said, was against the law. But what if I didn't, I asked: what would occur? She supposed, said my mother, we would be summonsed. I said, is that like sued? I had heard the word "sued." It sounded to me like the long, stinking hiss emitted when a tap was turned on the gas cooker, before the match was applied. Sued, gas: the words had a lower hiss than "marzipan," and long after they were spoken their trail lingered on the air, invisible, pernicious.

So there was no choice about going to St. Charles Borromeo; somehow I confused its compulsory nature with its permanent nature. One day, I thought, my mother would fail to collect me. She would "forget" and, tactfully, no one would remind her. I would be left at school and have to live there. My grandad would want to get me but a grandad is not in charge; he never comes to school. Even if my mother was on her way to retrieve me, she would be prevented by some accident, some stroke of fate. Thinking of this, my eyes began to leak tears which blurred my vision. Sometimes I yelled out with exasperation and fear of abandonment. Mrs. Simpson took off her tiny gold watch, and showed it to me. When the big hand, she said, and when the little hand, your mother will be here. She put her watch on her teacher's desk. The big girls and boys, who were already five, were allowed to bring me up and show it to me. I so hated their hands, their arms weighing down my neck, that I tried to cry silently, but a boy called Harry, who had blazing red hair, would call out, "She is crying, she is crying," whenever he saw tears dripping from my closed lids.

I thought I should be abandoned forever, in the Palace of Silly Questions. Do you want me to hit you with this ruler?

The children's favorite game was called Water. At the close of each afternoon, games were given out—paper, paints, crayons—and the most favored child of the day was called forward to the washbasin, which stood in the corner of the classroom. The pleasure of Water consisted of filling the basin and floating plastic ducks on it.

I got home and my handkerchief was damp. "Did you drop it down the toilet?" my mother said. She wasn't angry, which was a relief; these days I seemed to magnetize wrath. "No," I said. My voice was faint. "I had Water." How could she know the stultifying horror of those two yellow plastic ducks? Of thirty minutes in the company of said ducks? And that this was supposed to be a prize, a favor, an honor that made the children fume with envy, the unseen children at your back? Never turn your back on the enemy: any knight knows it. Worse, how could my mother think, how could she ever imagine, that I would use the school lavatories? A near approach had been enough for me, to those stinking closets under the shadow of a high wall, the ground running from the pipes that burst every winter, the wood of their doors rotting as if a giant rat had gnawed them from the ground up. We had an outside one at home, shared with no. 54: but excuse me, this? I had to go to what was called "the babies' lavatory," which was half-size. The trouble with the babies was, they were so very approximate in their arrangements; they didn't know the lavatory bowl from the floor.

So did she not know everything, my mother? I thought that was the setup, between mother and child. I understood a fair percentage of other people's thoughts, or at least the thoughts of the people to whom I was related, the people with whom I lived on Bankbottom; I understood outlying uncles who wheezed in, and could predict with a fair degree of success what they would say next. I assumed that comprehension was reciprocal. I understood my mother to understand me. I was devastated that the mere fact of being a mile up the road meant she didn't know what was going on in the infants' classroom.

I can't say I learned nothing, at St. Charles Borromeo. I learned bladder control; which is good for women, useful in later life. The second thing I learned was that I had got almost everything terribly wrong.

"Missus Simpson," Harry called out. "Ilary is crying again!"

A strange thing occurred. My mother's hair changed color. Once the tint of ashes, it was now a beautiful shade unknown in nature. The nearest you would come to it would be if—riding out one day in your blazoned surcoat, sword at your side, reins loose in your hands, the air mild—you observed from afar a slow fire within an autumn wood.

I may have taken some time to notice the change. Months, perhaps: functioning, as I did, on the level of the tabletop, and with my eyes turned inward. So peculiar was the occurrence, so estranging—so much what I would learn to call *unheimlich*—that I doubted the evidence of my senses and didn't trust my memory. When I plucked up courage, my voice faltered—"do you, have you . . . please, was your hair always that color?" With crushing certainty, my mother answered that I should never say such a thing. My memory was at fault! I wish I hadn't made her angry, standing in the kitchen at 56 Bankbottom. It wasn't my wish to make her angry, in fact it was far from my mind. I just needed to know whether I could trust myself, my perceptions of things, the evidence of my senses. The answer, obviously, was no.

I had a brother. I had completely failed to notice my mother's pregnancy, though I had been besotted by her loose satin gown of peacock blue: its iridescence, its deep square neck which showed to perfection her skin's ivory glow. I went to the maternity home with my father, Henry, in the shiny black car that was the Hadfield taxi, to bring the baby home. "Wait," Henry said: and then my mother appeared. She stood on the steps, poised, as if hovering for a photographer. She carried the shawled marvel as if it were a bag of eggs, her face tenderly downturned: on the way home to Bankbottom, I don't remember that anyone spoke. I thought it was rapture. I could have been wrong.

On a fine hot day in summer the new baby was christened. For the occasion I had a new dress, white and pale yellow, crisp as a wafer. We went up the carriage drive, beneath the grim and dripping trees, and emerged, on level ground, by the convent and the church. "Go in," said my mother, indicating the convent door. "Go in, and ask Sister Joseph if she would like to come and see your brother, Ian."

I did it. It was the only time I ever entered that building, ever crossed the threshold, and my eyes must have been so busy that they stripped the varnish from the chairs, stripped the paint from the walls: because later I would write a novel largely set in that convent. I found no one at first, no inhabited room, so I kept moving, into the innards of the place, until I found sundry nuns, perched—as it seemed to me—at high desks, in a room painted pale green. They were gray seamy nuns, with the complexions of creatures kept under stones. I thought that I must provide—in my sudden appearance, my wafer-crisp dress, and my important request—the highlight of their whiskery week, like an unlooked-for ray of grace. I said only what I had been told to say: "Would you like to come and see my brother, Ian?"

The church was dark, at any season; dark on a blazing August day. As the christening party gathered by the font, the only reflection came from the priest's shining pate and the startling white of his robe. The infant, huge in frills, was there to abjure the devil, but his bulk was lost in his godmother's rocking arms.

My mother approached the priest, who put into her hand a lighted candle. A look of understanding, I thought, passed between them. It was a secret look, and superior to anything I could comprehend. Her demeanor was demure, smiling, yet penitential. She held up the taper and turned away from the christening party. She turned her back and walked slowly into the body of the church, away from the light. I was alarmed, baffled. I didn't know why she should be going alone, without me by her side, her protector and knight. I wanted to run after her. But only my eyes followed the candle's flicker, and followed the upright figure, enveloped by darkness, kneeling at last by the center aisle: where she made, far from me, her own diffuse, particular light.

It was midwinter when my second and final brother was born. I have no memories of his christening. It is a whiteout; it is as if his first days are hidden from me, as if his first months of life are frozen in the deepest frost, inside a Russian doll with her fists sealed in her sleeves. I remember the summer that followed, when he convulsed in his pram, his tiny face blue under a blue, stormy August sky: how I put my hands on the pram's handle, rocking him, rocking him: but how he screamed, nevertheless, nevertheless, inconsolable, while the flies and bees buzzed and the storshions blowing their trumpets climbed the bamboo frames on the wall: but it was a different wall, a different house now, a different backdrop and enough to make anybody scream.

It was temper, people said, fanning their faces as his yells wound down to a whimper; it was only temper that made him howl. I thought it was being second, second boy. Or it was sleeping in our new upstairs, with its shady inhabitants: perhaps waking in the night and not knowing who was there, seeing a strange shape pass against the curtains and the street lamp. I thought it was being sent to earth in the depth of winter, and brought home swaddled to the strange house, which he had not known before he was born. God tempers the wind to the shorn lamb; this saying did not hold good, in Hadfield, Glossop, Near Manchester. By now, our lives had taken an interesting turn.

The Secret Garden

W hen I was a child we used to play with toys called
Magic Slates. There was a colored cardboard frame,
like a picture frame, which held a rectangle of carbon paper
covered by a sheet of clear plastic. You had a writing imple-
ment like a short knitting needle, with which you inscribed the
plastic sheet. Behind the clear panel, your secret writing
appeared; then you pulled up a cardboard tab, swished up the
"slate," and the marks vanished.

The magic slate was a favorite toy of mine. I could write
anything I liked, but if someone loomed into view I could
disappear it in an instant. I wrote many thoughts and observa-
tions, and letters from an imaginary me to an imaginary someone. I believed I was doing it in perfect safety. But one day the
light caught the surface at a certain angle, and when I held the
slate away from me and turned it I saw that the pen left marks
in the plastic sheet, like the tracks of writing on water. It would
have been possible, with some labor and diligence, to discover
the words even after they had been erased. After that I left aside
the Magic Slate. I didn't dare to risk it. Even now I have a horror of someone standing behind my desk and looking over my

shoulder as the words appear on the screen. There is a place, a gap, a hiatus, between the hatching words, flinching and raw, and those that are ready to take their place in the world, words that are ready to stand up and fight.

If people ask my advice about writing I say, don't show your work before you're ready. They understand this, and are glad to be given permission to be cautious. I should add, don't do your work before you're ready. Just because you have an idea for a story doesn't mean you're ready to write it. You may have to creep toward it, dwell with it, grow up with it: perhaps for half your lifetime. That piece of advice—to delay, hold off—is harder to accept. The obvious question is this: how can you tell when the moment has come? I have hesitated for such a long time before beginning this narrative. For a long time I felt as if someone else were writing my life. I seemed able to create or interpret characters in fiction, but not able to create or interpret myself. About the time I reached midlife, I began to understand why this was. The book of me was indeed being written by other people: by my parents, by the child I once was, and by my own unborn children, stretching out their ghost fingers to grab the pen. I began this writing in an attempt to seize the copyright in myself.

Perhaps I would have written it sooner if I had thought I could trust the Magic Slate, but after I was six or seven concealment became my habit. My thoughts remained in my head, multiplying, buzzing like bluebottles in a box.

If you stand at the end of our yard at Bankbottom, and look uphill, you can see the place where they're building the flats. They are two story, with pebble dash on the outside. They are a novelty, and novelty is suspect; few people in Hadfield have thought of living without stairs. There are council houses at the upper end of the settlement, built for people from Manchester who had been displaced by the war. "She comes from the council houses, you know," is the phrase used; which means, roughly, lock up your spoons. I guess the council houses have superior sanitation—indoor lavatories, hot water, baths perhaps—and the Hadfield people are always anxious to sneer at anyone who they think might be going soft.

My mother lights up with indignation when she speaks of the new flats, and her incandescent hair glows around her head. "It's scandalous! It's ridiculous! They're moving them in before the light fittings have been put up! No curtain rails between the lot of them."

I take Evelyn down to the end of the yard. I lead her in a game called Talking About the New Flats. We put our hands on our hips. We stare furiously over the wall (the very wall where Tibby used to run, Tibby the Protestant cat). We shout, "It's scandalous. It's ridiculous! No curtain rails between the lot of them!"

Evelyn tires of the game. She wants to play Ballet School. I stay on, shouting. I wonder if, really, my mother would like one of the flats. But no Catholics can get them; that is generally known.

A few weeks on, a little girl comes to our yard and says she is from the flats and wants to play. Her name is Heather. She is pretty and respectable, but what sort of name is that? A little boy comes. He is weedy and small. He begs to play with us. How can we refuse him? Evelyn asks passionately; his age is six and three quarters! His age does not impress me. I walk away. He runs after me and cries, and says if he can play with us he will do anything, we can hide and he will permanently seek. He will give us a penny if he can play with us: threepence. The more he raises the sum the more disdainful I appear. In the end I turn my back and walk away. Two women are standing on their back doorsteps and marvel at my hard sectarian heart. I say to Evelyn, over my shoulder, You play with him, if you want! I don't play with boys.

Boys are what I have to fight at school. If you can't join them, beat them. I am out of the babies' class and released from the stinking stone pen beside the latrines, out into the broad playground under the dripping trees. I come home and say, "Grandad, a big boy hit me." He says, "Lovie, now I'll teach you how to fight." He teaches fair tactics, nothing low. But when the next fight comes, I walk away with a different result. It's too easy! Punch to solar plexus, big boy folds. His head is within range. "As you please now," Grandad says: "Keep it easy, no need to make a fist. Try a big slap across the chops." I do it. Tears spring from the eyes of the big boy. He reels, clutching his diaphragm, away from the railings. Oh Miss, she hit me, she hit me!

I am amazed: less by my performance, than by his; his alarming wails, his bawls. I don't want to do this again unless I have to, I decide. In only a year I will have to go to confession and learn to examine my conscience. What I am experiencing is the beginning of compunction; but is it the awakening of a sense of sin, or is it the beginning of femininity? Do boys have compunction? I don't think so. Knight errants? They have compunction for all the weak and oppressed. Shame is somewhere among my feelings about this incident. I don't know who it belongs to: to me, or the boy I've beaten, or some ghostly, fading boy I still carry inside.

Later, when I am a big girl, ten years old, a true bully arises in our own class. He is a short boy with shorn hair, and his name is Gary, which is a bully name if ever you heard one. He is broad, white, muscled, compact, and made of rubber. He takes my beret and throws it in the ditch. I declare I will make war on him. You can't bash Gary C.! the little girls say. I go after him, pale with fury, spitting with wrath. He stands his ground. I strike out. My fists sink into his torso and bounce back. The feeling is curiously soothing. I need have no conscience about him. He's made of some substance denser than flesh. I suppose he hits me back, but it doesn't hurt. By now, ten, I am disconnecting from my body. It has no capabilities and no capacities, except to be in the way, to be where it's not wanted. Gary's like a creature the knight meets in a forest, you lop its head off and it regrows. He's a monster. My breath comes hard, my heart hammers. I'm trapped in a joke with no space between the setup and the punch line. *Thud, thud, thud.* "Have you heard this one?" *Thud, thud, thud.* "Two monsters are having a boxing match."

For a while, at six, I cling to the prospect of a man's life. I play with the cleverest girl in the class, whose name is Jacqueline. Naturally she takes the name Jack, and I am Bill. The game is called Men, and the good thing is that even when we aren't actually playing it we can use these secret names. But Jacqueline tells me, "You don't talk like us," and stops bothering with me. Of course I don't talk like them; they are a race of varlets, base knaves, and curs. I begin bothering with the Italian children, and the ones who at home speak refugees' languages, a flax-blond Ukrainian child and a huddle of darned and desolate Poles. I try to interest another girl in the game of Men. She is a shy, speechless child called Margaret, whose face is permanently scarlet from some inner humiliation. As her name she selects "Walter." It is what her father is called. I can't explain why this is no good. "Walter," it proves, never does anything manly. The whole excitement is confined to "Walter comes home for his tea." So the game of Men is left off.

It is time for me to take up skipping instead. I don't want to but I have to try. I'd rather turn the rope and say the rhyme than skip. In hopscotch, another game, I should have the advantage because I have such beautiful stones to skim. One day before I was born (so my mother says) my grandmother took against the marble washstand, blaming it for being old-fashioned. She ordered it out of the house and said to my grandad, "Smash it up, George!" Pieces of marble are still embedded in the dirt of the backyard. I dig them up and they make hopscotches that are heavy in the hand, white as a rock of sugar and smooth as ice. Where do they go, these wonderful stones? I suppose I give them away, so that people will leave me alone. The game is better than skipping, but I find that when I try to stand on one leg, the pressure of my thoughts pushes me over.

Evelyn and I get a football and kick it at the coal sheds. She would like to be Manchester United, but I explain that Protestants can only be Manchester City. She wins, all the same; the days of playing Ballet School, without me, have left her fleet-footed. But what does it profit her? She has to go to Brownies. She has to get her Darning Badge. She can't darn. She weeps in frustration just thinking about it. Evelyn has a party for her sixth birthday. There are two guests, her and me. We get overexcited and knock over our fizzy drinks: or rather, I do. Our drink is called Cyd-Apple: related to cider, but for those of a small age. I think about the glass I lost, and feel aggrieved. Later in life I drink cider, but the dry, still taste is musty, as if the glass had been kept in a cupboard for twenty years.

Overexcited is bad, fidget is bad; obedient is good. Mr. and Mrs. Aldous have a television set. I go down to watch the children's serial. It is *The Secret Garden*. The curtains are pulled, so the black-and-white picture stands out more; we lie on the rug, chins on our hands, like children in picture books, like illustrations of ourselves. We don't fidget at all, but I live in terror that Mr. Aldous will come home before the end of the episode, will grow in from the street with his nodular, fibrous arms. At the end of many weeks I have saved up the entire story. I go home and announce it to my mother: *The Secret Garden,* here is that story. It spools out and out of my mouth, narrative, dialogue, and commentary. She looks stunned. We are in the kitchen, but not the kitchen at Bankbottom. This is Brosscroft, another house entirely.

After the disappointment over the flats, my mother says, "I'm getting us a house!" She goes to the bank for her savings. We go uphill to Brosscroft. My mother says, This is the house I have got.

There are steps up to the massive front door. Inside everything is painted in dark green. The kitchen has bare stone flags. There are gas mantles on the wall.

When I go there again, it is the day we move in. I am moving in with my mother and father and brother Ian, my younger brother being still unborn. It takes five minutes to run down the hill to Bankbottom, but still, it is a change and I am not sure I am prepared for it. The house is no longer dark green. The front room has striped wallpaper, gray and white with a pinstripe of what we call maroon. The color of the paintwork, my mother says, is French beige. There is a huge old-fashioned range in the front room, but my mother says she'll soon get that knocked out. As in my grandmother's house, we will only heat one room. Hot water is got by boiling kettles. But the lavatory is our own, and is not exactly outside either; it is just off a drafty stone-flagged room called "the Glass Place," behind the kitchen. There is a private yard with a patch of grass, and high walls up which the storshions will grow. Beyond the yard is a garden. It is huge, my mother says, with the fields beyond it. When it is cleared we will be able to understand its dimensions. At the moment, the tangled bushes are head-high, when your head's as high as mine. I can't even see to the end of it.

The night we move in, the big square kitchen is a patch of light, yellow light against the chaos outside. There is chill in the air, and my mother is busy at the table, putting together a first meal. Henry, she says, the knife! It is the black-handled knife, the bread knife, with its hair-thin blade. It has been left behind at Bankbottom; and that is my knife, she says.

It is true. It is the knife I am used to seeing in her hand. Henry strides out, into the blue twilight, in his black-and-white tweed coat. My mother goes to the new stove, and then peers into the dark cupboard where the gas meter is kept. The gas is turned off, she says, I will have to—No! I say. I stop her hand. I beg her. No, no, don't do it. Don't turn on the gas before my daddy comes back. Gas, sue, sue, gas, hiss, hiss, bang. I am begging and beseeching. I can't tell her my reason. Please no, wait for him, let him do it, please: it's for men. I am in the first killing crisis of my life and unable to explain how to avert it. She looks at me, a long, considering look: "All right," she says. I am as astonished as she was, when I recited the entire *Secret Garden* at a stroke. All right? I take a breath. I can hardly believe any adult will take notice of me, I can scarcely believe our lives are to be saved.

I am slightly afraid that, anyway, the house will blow up; in that case, we will all explode together. But when Henry comes back, cheerful and chilled, the knife under his jacket, *alles in Ordnung*. Man switches on gas. No one sued. No one dead. No mysterious escapes, no invisible presences.

Mum pins an Elvis picture on the kitchen wall. Elvis is in his army uniform. Every day I see his fat-lipped sloe-eyed dumbness. It's not what you do, I think; you should like your husband best. I know it's all wrong, all gone wrong: and going worse, day by day.

I am beside myself with interest in the baby, Ian. I tap on the side of his pram a certain rhythm, like rudimentary code, child to child: dot-dot-dot-dot? He turns his blue eyes on me, and taps back: dash dash. Lying on his back, he kicks out the rhythm with his heels. "This baby has almost kicked his pram through," my mother says in horror, "with the pounding of his great powerful feet." When he tries to walk, I support him like an old comrade with a battlefield casualty, propping him under his armpits when he sags. His knees point outward, his legs bow under the power of his body, and I bounce him back on course by the straps of his romper suit: Frog, March to the Frying Pan! I sing. I don't know why. I have heard of it as a song, and it seems apt. I don't have any ill will toward him: only the opposite. He becomes my occupation, my hobby, my cause. I have heard of children who are jealous: I am sure that is not me. People laugh that if he falls on me he will kill me. I am a tiny doll creature with red smiling lips, stick limbs, and fair hair: an innocent abroad, a dumb broad, a feather on the breath of God.

When I am six years old I am put to bed in my parents' room at Brosscroft. So far only one bedroom of the house is habitable.

The baby's cot stands against the window wall, the double bed occupies the center of the room, my small cream-painted bed is nearest the door. I lie under a tartan rug and my fingers twist and plait its fringe; plait, untwist, plait again: the wool is rough against my fingertips. I will myself into dreaming; I think about Red Indians and about Jesus, because Jesus is a thing I am exhorted to think about and I try, I do try. I think about my teepee, my tomahawk, my stocky bay horse who is standing even now, a striped blanket thrown over his back, ready to gallop me over the plains, into the red and dusty west. Then I think about how, downstairs perhaps even at this moment, my mother is putting on her coat and picking up her bag.

I believe she will leave in the night, abandon me. We should never have come to this house; we should have stayed as we were, with Grandma and Grandad down at Bankbottom. Everything has gone wrong, so wrong that I don't know how to express it or understand it; I know that anyone who can flee disaster should do so, leaving the weak, the old, and the babies behind in the wreckage. My mother is smart and fit and I think she will run, and take her chance on another life, a better life elsewhere: some princess place, where her real family lives. With her ready smiles and her glowing sunset head, she does not belong here, in these enclosing shadows: in these rooms that have filled silently with unseen, hostile observers.

My father puts the baby to bed; this hour, when he is upstairs with the baby and me, seems like the time she would run. I think that, although it will almost kill me, I can bear it if I know the moment she goes, if I hear the front door close after her. But I can't bear it if I go downstairs in the morning to a cold and empty kitchen—warmed only by Elvis, his fat face glowing like the rising sun.

So I lie awake, listening, long after my father has crept

downstairs, listening by the glow of the nightlight to the sounds of the house. In the morning I am too tired to get up, but I must go to school or else I will be sued. My arms and legs ache with a singing pain. The doctor says it is growing pains. One day I find I cannot breathe. The doctor says if I didn't think about breathing I'd be able to do it. Frankly, he's sick of being asked what's wrong with me. He calls me Little Miss Neverwell. I am angry. I don't like being given a name. It's too much like power over me.

Persons shouldn't name you. Rumpelstiltskin.

Jack comes to visit us. He comes for his tea. These teas seem to be separate extra meals, in the big kitchen when the lights are on and the wild gardens fade into a dark bloom. We cook strange, frivolous dishes: dip eggs suddenly into bubbling fat, so that they fizz up like sea creatures, puff into pearls with translucent whitish legs. Is Jack coming today? I ask. Oh good. I am looking for someone to marry. It's a business I want to get settled up. I hope Jack might do, though it is a pity he is not my relative. He is just someone we know.

Down at Bankbottom, they are talking about the latest novelty from Rome: the pope says you can marry your second cousin! That means, people say, that Ilary could marry . . . if she wanted, of course . . . then they turn up various names of people I haven't heard of. I wish I had heard of them: I am keen for intelligence of these candidates; I am, I already know, the kind of person who would marry back into my own family, to keep us all together, to guarantee me a supply of familiar people, great-uncles needing Cheshire cheese, great-aunts with hats discussing in low voices while wielding their spoons over bowls of tinned peaches. I have a great-uncle who was in a military prison, "our Joe he is red-hot Labour," my grandmother says; I have a great-aunt who for money sold her long golden hair. Why are they great-uncles and great-aunts? Where is the next generation? Where are their children? Never born, or dead as babies. Poverty, my mother says, pneumonia. I write down, "pneumonia." I don't know it is an illness, I think it is a cold wind that blows.

One day Jack comes for his tea and doesn't go home again. "Is he never going home?" I say. Night falls, on this new dispensation; it falls and falls on me. In subsequent weeks I become enraged, and am thrown into the Glass Place. Jack and my mother sit in the kitchen. I jump at the kitchen window and make faces at them. They draw the curtains and laugh. I try to crash the back door, but they have bolted it.

I stamp and rage, outside in the cold. Rumpelstiltskin is my name.

You should not judge your parents. Mostly—this is the condition of parents—they were doing the best they could. They were addled and penniless and couldn't afford lawyers, they were every man's hand against them, they were—when you do the arithmetic—pathetically young. They couldn't see the wood for the trees or the way through the week from Monday to Friday. They were in love or they were enraged, they were betrayed or bitterly, bitterly disappointed, and just like our own generation they clutched at any chance to make it right, to make a change, to get a second chance: they beat off the fetters of logic and they gathered themselves up in weakness and despair and they spat in the eye of fate. This is what parents do. They believe love conquers all, or why would they have children, why would they have you? You should not judge your parents.

When you are six, seven, you do not know this. I feel that I myself have been judged: that I have committed an unnamed offense: that I have been sentenced, and that some unspecified penalty will be exacted, at short notice. Sued, gas, sued, hiss, dead.

This is the worst time in my life: days of despair. I am back on the pier at Blackpool, with the screaming gulls and the wind, looking down into the boiling sea. Words swirl over my head, words of loathing and contempt. A great hand lifts me; it is the hand of the law. And here is my punishment, coming now, coming now; I feel the rush of air against my face. The law lifts me up into the wind, the law lets me go; I fall through space, and on the rocks my head smashes open like an egg. The sea drinks my yellow blood.

On a Saturday morning at Brosscroft I come down early and to my surprise Grandad is there. He is in the stone-shelved pantry, where the air is cold even in August. His tools are laid out there, because he's been helping fix up the house, but now he is wiping them and slotting them away in their canvas cradles. "What are you doing, Grandad?" I say. He says, "Sweetheart, I am packing these up, and going home."

I walk away, my heart sinking.

In the kitchen my mother grabs me. "What did he say to you?"

"Nothing."

"What?" She is burning, her cheeks flushed, her hair a conflagration. "Nothing? You mean he didn't speak to you?"

I see some furious new row in the making. I answer, without spirit, taking refuge in the literal: like the stupid messenger, bringing the bad news twice. "He said what he was doing. He said, sweetheart, I am packing these up, and going home."

Grandad walks away, down to Bankbottom, his spine

unyielding, his neck stiff. Somewhere in the house a door slams. Glass trembles in its frames. Cupboards creak, the new mirror in the front room rattles its chain against its nail. The stairhead is lightless, the dead center of the house. I think I see someone turning the corner, down the corridor to the bedroom where my father, Henry, now sleeps in a single bed. The walls are yellow in that room and the curtains half-drawn.

What happens now? We are talked about in the street. Some rules have been broken. A darkness closes about our house. The air becomes jaundiced and clotted, and hangs in gaseous clouds over the rooms. I see them so thickly that I think I am going to bump my head on them.

Now the two boys sleep in the main bedroom, the largest in my cream bed and the smallest in his cot. I am moved into my father's room, which is the yellow room down the passage. There is no natural light in the passage, only an overhead bulb that, by casting shadows, seems to thicken the murk rather than disperse it. I never walk but run between the stairhead and my bed. Our two puppies cry in the night. They are frightened. The man who comes to paint the stairhead is frightened, but I am not supposed to overhear about that.

The door key is missing. The house is turned over for it. Every surface is checked and every drawer. The floor is crawled with padding hands and sensitive knees. All visitors—but there are not many—have their brains trounced about it and their movements thoroughly interrogated. Some two days pass, and the key returns, placed on top of the china cabinet, dead center.

My mother stops going out to the shops. Only my godmother comes and goes between our house and Bankbottom. The children at school question me about our living arrangements, who sleeps in what bed. I don't understand why they want to know but I don't tell them anything. I hate going to school. Often I am ill with my growing pains and the breathing I am not supposed to think about and the high fever that is the same as I had in Blackpool, and raging headaches that leave me hollow-eyed. When I go back to school after a few days nobody seems to know me and behind my own back I have gone up a class. The new teacher is called Miss Porter. I don't understand how she writes down the arithmetic. I've missed something. I put up my hand and say I don't understand. She stares at me in incredulity. Don't understand? Don't understand? What broil or civil mutiny is this? Why don't I just copy from the child next to me, like all the other little sillies? "You don't understand?" she repeats, her eyes popping with indignation. There is an outbreak of screeching giggles and adenoidal snorting.

Miss Porter is gone very soon. My ignorance remains.

Summer comes: my grandparents take me on a day trip to Blackpool. Along the promenade there are glass-walled shelters, with benches; it is in these that visitors spend most of their summers, shrinking from the wind and rain. I have no sooner set my foot on the pavements of the town than I begin to shiver and burn. My eyes close against the light and I feel as if their surfaces have been scrubbed with sand. I spend the long afternoon of a rare sunny day, stretched full length on one of the benches with my head on my grandmother's lap; my new straw basket, with its bright daisy pattern, lies useless by my side. When I get home it is discovered that I am incubating measles. A year or two later, we will go to Blackpool *en famille,* in Jack's car. That evening I will return to Brosscroft semiconscious, the stars spinning over my head as they lift me, limp, from the backseat, and carry me up the steps to the house.

We will have our days out in Southport after that, the car deep in the sand dunes, morosely cooking chips over a Primus stove.

After Miss Porter went, a person new to the school took over the class. Let us call her Mrs. Stevens; she was a ginger creature with bristling hair and prominent shinbones. She was also a Protestant. This was a peculiar thing, a Protestant teacher. Someone else had to teach us catechism, which occupied the first hour of the day. It was a soft and sweet subject; on the blackboard you drew an M on top of a W, which made the shape of the wings of an angel, and was to remind you that an angel was a Mind and a Will.

What came next was much cruder. At ten o'clock Mrs. Stevens charged in, bristling. She swung from her fist a big tartan shopping bag; though the tartan was, I suppose, unknown to any clan. On that first day, we were unprepared for the whirlwind that was to tear us up. Mrs. Stevens didn't know our names. She didn't know our provenance. She didn't know the thing that we held in reverence, which was called Where We Are Up To. Our squared books were given out as usual. They kept our sums running carefully down the page, the faint blue lines squaring off the hundreds, the tens, and the units. But Mrs. Stevens didn't agree with columns. We had to work the sums horizontally, just as they were printed in our textbook. At the sight of vertical jotting, however surreptitious, she shot down the aisle and slapped you.

Mrs. Stevens wrote on the board "Problems"; and after it, a short story without a climax or moral. A man goes into a shop and buys fruit, a man fills a bucket, a man takes a train to a station to a distance of fifteen miles. A woman never did anything, you observed at once; and it wasn't a story; it wasn't a joke: it was—breathe it!—a sum. The knowledge penetrated the classroom in a low despairing hiss, spreading from the mites at the back to the one at the front. "No talking!" cried Mrs. Stevens. People began to cry. They began to knuckle their little heads. She didn't even print, but did Real Writing, which is what we called it when you joined the letters: and we weren't up to joining up! When it came to the part of the day called Reading, she expected us to follow when one child read out loud, and take up where he left off. Previously, we had thought of reading as a private activity, perhaps shared with the teacher, perhaps sweated over alone. But now it was to be communal. Communal was not much use, when some of us were up to Far & Wide Reader Green Book Four, while others were still mastering Letters up to D.

My first opinion of Mrs. Stevens was that she was insane. My grandfather had told me that an ancestor of his had once walked the whole night, over the Derbyshire moors, with a man he later discovered to be an escaped lunatic. When I found that Mrs. Stevens, who like me went home for her dinner, was in the habit of wending down Woolley Bridge Road at ten minutes past one, I would join her and say, "Miss, can I carry your bag?" I was interested by the way she had to force herself to smile. No anatomical operations seemed mechanical to me. I was interested by the way her shinbones went before the rest of her legs, the calf muscle flapping behind.

I suppose that, if there'd been anyone around to see, carrying her bag might have seemed sycophantic. So far as I was concerned, it was a diagnostic ploy. It had no bearing on the way she treated me, once we got back to the schoolroom: shouting and hitting. But on those journeys, she didn't talk to me; I talked to her. "Oh yes?" she would say, and "Oh have you?"

These minimal responses seemed correct, from her thin lips. I don't know what I told her. My thoughts on God? How to spell Worcester? God and strange spellings were my preoccupations, around that time.

There are plenty of teachers, I am sure, who pretend to like children and don't. Mrs. Stevens didn't even pretend. My mother, who was interested in my progress, took a periodical called *Child Education*. Sometimes, for my benefit, she pinned up dull little pictures out of it, monochrome beside the flagrant bronze of Elvis. Mrs. Stevens also had access to this magazine, and while we sat dumbfounded she read us articles out of it, about tadpoles and caterpillars. This was called Nature Study. It was good enough for grubs like us; outside, the rain hissed down on moorland and street, and small drenched things scuttled for cover, on two legs or four.

In those days—which to people born after the 1950s must seem impossibly deprived and frightening, like the days of the Holy Inquisition—children were forbidden from speaking for most of the hours of the school day, unless they were asked a direct question, and thus required and indeed commanded to speak. Mrs. Stevens introduced a further disability: if our hands were not employed in some specific, authorized activity, we were to sit with our arms folded behind our backs. This posture—which is as near as you can get to a natural straitjacket—drove me to an extreme of tearful frustration. It shackled my brain and bound my hands, separated my Mind from my Will. I came home and said, she ought not to be able to do it. But no one can have been listening; they were listening to something else, at the time.

Soon I no longer carried her bag or walked with her down the road to school. Instead I followed her, a shadow, watching her faded ginger head bob above the collar of her coat that pretended to be fur: like a head on a platter. At first we children had talked about her, in amazed and pitiful tones; then we stopped talking. We were drawn, as a group, as a class, into a shamed secrecy, observing how she liked to drag up the boys' short trousers to slap the tops of their thighs, and pull up the girls' skirts; there was a buzz in the air which was not innocent. She would threaten us with a "twankey," which I thought must be some Protestant word; I understood what she meant, though. Once she shouted at a child to "bend over," in front of the class, and I noted how his spine became wood, and he was incapable of obeying or not obeying. She shouted the command again, then slapped him anyway.

Children were beaten, in our village, sometimes grotesquely. I was hardly out of the babies' class when on a Monday morning a little girl with a face the color of paper whispered to me, "On Sat'day our dad beat our Ann till she bled." And I knew our Ann, who was like her younger sister a child so pallid and frail that you wouldn't think there was any blood inside her. I felt my man's spirit aroused, my ardor clenching inside my chest like a fist within a mailed glove. Saddle my charger: I'll canter up their street and decapitate him. My sword arm twitched, and I pictured one lazy, scything stroke, myself hardly breaking sweat; then the head, bouncing downhill over the cobbles. I sat shivering, my eyes closed, behind my table; I was six and the lesson was sums, the day sunny. In Hadfield, as everywhere in the history of the world, violence without justification or apology was meted out by big people to small. But there were rules. Strangers didn't hit you, only your family. Protestants didn't hit you, they had no authority over you; that was (in my mind) an established fact of life. I saw that the situation was impossible, and that if necessary Mrs. Stevens would have to be slain.

As soon as I thought this, my fear became extreme. I trembled when she spoke to me; but what made me even more queasy than my own fear was the fear she inspired in others. I don't know if there is a case on record of a child of seven murdering a schoolteacher, but I think there ought to be, and in a way I would respect myself much more if I had done the deed; I was determined, already, to distinguish myself in my generation. But picture my situation. I am seven and becoming realistic. I know I cannot act alone. As long as a year ago, I had given up the possibility of forming a band of gallant knights, or even mustering a company of men-at-arms, to lie in wait behind the hedgerows, to swoop down between the black trees above the church.

I am seven, only seven. Fever hits me again, knocking me out of the saddle. I rise from bed each time more etiolated, my eyes paler. My hair is growing again, but I know it is always under threat when the thermometer begins to creep up the scale. To console me for being an invalid, I get "Alice" to read. I read both her adventures but I prefer the Looking Glass. It is easy to imagine myself passing through a mirror, every cell of my body thinning, stretching, becoming transparent, forming and re-forming in some other dimension.

The three households are still divided, 56 and 58 Bankbottom against 20 Brosscroft. I come and go, eating my morning toast at Brosscroft, having my midday dinner at Bankbottom with Grandma, and at the end of the school day, swaying and fatigued, climbing the hill to have my tea in the Brosscroft kitchen, listening out for the front door, for the sound of my father, Henry, sliding in, for the squeak of the handbrake as Jack's car pulls up on the hill outside. No one quarrels, no one cries—only me; no words are exchanged; the situation remains unspoken, indefinite. My godmother brings the meat and the loaves, because my mother no longer goes to the butcher or the baker; she makes do with the Brosscroft corner shop, where the proprietor is kind. She no longer goes to Mass on Sunday, or indeed anywhere at all. In the evening she and Jack occupy the big kitchen, my father the front room; but mostly the men seem to time their comings and goings to miss each other. At the weekend Jack goes out and hacks savagely at the undergrowth of the garden, till he has hacked it down and the view is plain, from the Glass Place at the back of the kitchen to the crumbling back fence, to the fields beyond, and beyond the fields the rising ground of the moors. When the weather is wet, he strips off wallpaper and burns away layers of paint. He works in a fury, his sallow muscular body dripping with sweat.

But the spirits gather thickly in the half-finished house, falling from their places in the glass-fronted cupboards to the right of the fireplace, waking and stretching from their sooty slumbers behind the demolished range. They discharge from the burnt walls in puffs, they are scraped into slivers as the old wallpaper peels away, and lie curled on the floors, mocking the bristle brush. Our daily life is hushed, driven into corners. We move in a rush between the house's safe areas, and the ones less safe, where, as you enter a room, you get the impression that someone is waiting for you. The dogs, who are no longer puppies, squeal with fear in the night. My mother comes down to them, shivering in her nightdress, and sees their hackles raised, their thin forms shrinking against the dawn light. One night, I hear my mother and Jack, discussing. I am lurking in the cold Glass Place, coming in from the lavatory. "Well," she says, "so? So what do you think it is?" Her voice rises, in an equal blend of challenge, fear, and scorn. "What do you think it is? Ghosts?"

She has spoken my thoughts: which I thought were unspeakable. The hairs rise on the back of my neck. I do not know the word "horripilation." But imagine how pleased I would be, if I did.

Outside the house, what passes for life goes on. I am seven, I have reached the age of reason. Like every other little Catholic body, I must take the sacraments, Penance and Holy Communion. No problem! I am great in theology.

I had begun practicing as a parish priest at five years old. I used to walk with measured tread the length of the backyard, my eyes cast down, my hands folded over my heart, and I would tap sadly at Annie Connor's back door, and say, Mrs. Connor, now, I've come for your Confession. I believe there's something you're very sorry for, and I'm just here now to forgive you.

"Oh come in, Father," she would say. "Would you like a chocolate biscuit?" Then, rolling her eyes in penitence, "Oh, Father, I have been swearing!"

"Now that's very well, Mrs. Connor," I would say, "but didn't you say the same last month?"

"I did, I did," she would admit. "But Father, don't be too hard, for I've a lot to make me swear."

The doctrine of transubstantiation caused me no headache. I was not surprised to find that a round wafer was the body of Jesus Christ. I'd been saying for years that things like this occurred, if people would only notice. Spaniel and cow fused their nature, so did man and plant: look at Mr. Aldous, his milky stalks for arms. Girl could change to boy: though this had not happened to me, and I knew now it never would.

When the day of Holy Communion came, I was amazed at how the body of Christ pasted itself to my front teeth and furred my hard palate. It was like eating smog. Saint Catherine of Siena said that when she took the host into her mouth she could feel the bones of Jesus crunching between her teeth. She must have been a very imaginative sort of nun.

It was a good thing I'd been studying for the priesthood. Otherwise, it was a great deal to take in at one go: the knowledge of the black soul wiped clean at Confession, but then dirtying itself, by the mere accident of thought, by the time you were five minutes down the road from church. "Mrs. Connor," I'd say, "can you think of another sin?"

But then my great-aunt would reach out and grip my hands, and we'd be jumping and singing:

> *Oh I met with Napper Tandy and he took me by the hand,*
> *He said how is Old Ireland, and how does old Ireland*
> * stand?*
> *It's the most distressful countree, that ever yet was seen,*
> *They're hanging men and women for the wearing of the*
> * green.*

For a long time, I thought Napper Tandy was something like a great-uncle. I thought he might show his face one day, creaking up from the bus stop and wanting a sandwich.

Once I'd got the other side of the sacraments, I found that trying to be good wore me out and frayed my temper. It involved scrupulous vigilance, over your thoughts as well as your conduct, and it went on for all the hours that you were awake, and struck in again if you woke in the night. I was spiritually ambitious: sure route to failure, but I didn't know it then. I wanted an unspotted soul, a soul edged with light, like a clean but open window. It must be achieved, I thought, in calm, in stillness: as if the window opened over a blue lake, with white gulls gliding. It must be achieved among quiet people, whose speech was rare and thoughtful, whose every action was considered. I missed my grandad's methodical ways, and wished he would bring them back to Brosscroft, where the phantoms flapped and churned the air. For each task—turning mattresses, making pickles, mending a shoe—he would put on the appropriate apron, black or white canvas. He hummed as he worked, a civil hiss under his breath. He had retired from the railways, got his gold watch. It was an honorable retirement, and as an amateur pursuit, he stoked the Co-op boiler; I visited him, in the shadowy underground cavern that housed it, stinking like hell's antechamber. You reached it by turning off the ordinary street and descending surprisingly few steps; but you had to know it was there, for only his authorized assistants could find the door. I didn't take hellfire seriously. I had some idea what would be the extent of the devil's coal bill.

Sometimes, of an evening, he patrolled down the road to amuse himself with the boiler at the Hadfield Conservative Club, to cast an eye over its workings. He was a man in excellent standing, and as he strolled about the streets—which, unlike the rest of the family, he did freely—he met other elderly men who, breaking their own stately pace, would tip their caps to him and say, "How dost, Judd?" Then they might cross the road, and speak of boilers they had stoked, engines that had run sweetly: machine guns that had never jammed, thanks to the oiled ministrations of Sergeant Foster. Their voices summoned the pliant squeak of leather, the click of metal peg into its greased groove, and the dense smell of alien soil.

In a bar somewhere in the near east, Judd Foster sat down with a man called Kemal Ataturk, who told him what he meant to do for his native country. In Jerusalem, he was requested to join an ancient lodge of Freemasons: which he refused, rather shocked. He sailed into St. Paul's Bay on a Sunday morning;

peals of bells rang out over the waters, and as he looked up he saw the faithful hurrying to Mass, down the steep hills between the white houses. It is a sight, he said, I shall never forget. In the zoo at Cairo, he saw the rhinoceros.

Now he went about the house at Bankbottom, subdued and orderly, and as he worked it was Catholic hymns he sang to himself: "Mother of Christ, star of the sea, pray for the wanderer, pray for me." In my earlier childhood, I assisted him (as he was a convert) by carrying about a big wooden crucifix that I'd found in a bedroom cupboard. "I'm just practicing, Grandad," I'd say, "for when I'm an altar boy and I've to carry this at Corpus Christi."

In his religion there was Harvest Festival. Someone had told me that it was pagan. Pagans and heathens were a dubious thing altogether, condemned to a state called limbo when they passed away, together with all the little babies who died before they were baptized, of pneumonia and other causes: that cold wind that blows, that blows away salvation. It was not fair but life was not fair. Life is not bloody fair: so Jack says. Jack shouts: he feels ill used by fate. When he visited us at first, he used to stand in the kitchen at Brosscroft and play his mouth organ, leg kicking in time to the beat. He didn't regard Elvis, smirking behind him on the wall. Jack is a Protestant, or at least not a Catholic; this doesn't seem to bother my mother. In the army, he says, you had to give your religion. You couldn't say, none: if you did, they put you down as C of E.

He tells me a story while my mother combs out the tangles in my hair. His voice shakes, he is nervous. Like me, like the dogs, he is always listening, straining to catch a footstep overhead, a sound at the door. The whites of his eye are yellowish, round the mild caramel of his pupils; he has had jaundice, my mother says. One day, when I am standing outside the front door to have my photograph taken, in my white dress for one of the Feasts of the Church, a Protestant boy across the road points and jeers at me. Jack flies across the street as if he were launched off a springboard. He is snarling, his arm drawn back, the thick edge of his hand like a hatchet. The boy backs off, holds up his hands; he runs. Jack recrosses the road, scowling, purposive; I omit to thank him. So that, I think, is what it would be like if I were Jack's little girl.

Once a year, at school and church, we had Mission Sunday, when we sang about Africans and Indians. We called them Black Babies, and collected money for them. If you did well enough with fund-raising, you were allowed to own one. You could name it: I named my baby "Corinne," a choice found perverse, and, I suspect, scrubbed out from the forms immediately I turned my back. Clare Boylan has written a novel about a Black Baby who returns in later life to look up her owner. So I won't write another: only say that during the week before Mission Sunday we sang special hymns, their tunes undistinguished but their words thrilling. "For the infant wives and widows, Babies hurried to their graves . . ." How old did you need to be, to qualify as an infant wife? How did widowhood follow? And were the "babies hurried to their graves" the wives themselves, or their children?

The fact is, I might have got the words wrong; I may be producing some travesty of what was on the hymn sheet. At eight, I give up hearing. Whenever anyone speaks to me I say, "What?" While, irritated, they are repeating themselves, I gather myself, and recall to order the scattered pieces of my attention. Words are a blur to me; a moth's wing, flitting about the lamp of meaning. My own thoughts go at a different speed from that of human conversation, about two and a half times as fast, so I am always scrambling backward through people's speech, to work out which bit of which question I am supposed to be answering. I continue my habit of covert looking, out of the corner of my eye, and take up the art of sensing through the tips of my fingers. The chess pieces now hop to my command. Henry and I sit by lamplight, in the front room of the house at Brosscroft. Babies upstairs are snorting in their sleep, my mother and Jack have gone—where? Gone dancing? I don't know. My long father sits folded into his chair, pushing wearily at a pawn; till on one inspired night, I "castle" him, shuttling my king across two squares and bringing my rook into powerful, threatening play, grabbing the game's advantage; and he leans forward, fascinated, and says, did you *know* you were allowed to do that? The truth is between yes and no. I am eight and not such a fool as I appear. I am hardly incapable of studying the game, studying it sneakily, to confound my own daddy; though I'd prefer he thinks the move has come to me out of the blue, and I smile with dazzled surprise, as my rook, sprung from its corner, moving like a tank across country, picks off his best defenders. It is important not to try to win; to be casual; to be easy. In the same way, carelessly, he leaves his library books for me to read: his yellow-jacketed Gollancz. I read Arthur Koestler, *Reflections on Hanging.* I learn from it; I incorporate it into my dreams. I dream I have murdered someone. It is better to know about the penalty, than not.

Everybody laughs at me, because I can't hear, because I say "What?" My mother puts money on a horse called Mr. What. It wins the Grand National.

In the days when I was still seven, after the first Confession, the first Communion, I walked to school down Woolley Bridge Road, with the sooty hedgerow on my left and the wall on my right, and beyond that wall the canning factory, where the slurries of unimaginable meats were processed into tins. My Guardian Angel followed, half a step behind, always and invisibly at my left shoulder. And God walked with me, I thought he did. You would imagine that I asked Him to show Himself and put an end to the events at Brosscroft: the slammings of doors in the night, the great gusts of wind that roared through the rooms. But my idea of God was different. He was not a magician and should not be treated in that way; should not be asked to alter things and fix things, like some plumber or carpenter, like my grandad with his tools rolled in their canvas cradles. I had come to my own understanding of grace, the seeping channel between persons and God: the slow, green, and silted canal, between a person and the god inside them. Every sense is graceful, an agent of grace: touch, smell, taste. The grace of music is not for a child who says, "What?" My mother never plays the piano now, my father seldom; Jack is never seen to sit down to it, no doubt because he's C of E. And I can't carry a tune; I'm told brutally about this. I can't sing fa sol la ti do without singing flat. You can pray for grace, but it is a thing that creeps in unexpectedly, like a draft. It is a thing you can't plan for. By not asking for it, you get it. For one year, I carried this knowledge, and carried a simple space for God inside me: a jagged space surrounded by light, a waiting space cut out of my solar plexus. I subsisted in this watchful waiting, a readiness. But what came wasn't God at all.

Sometimes you come to a thing you can't write. You've written everything you can think of, to stop the story getting here. You know that, technically, your prose isn't up to it. You say then, very well: at least I know my limitations. So choose simple words; go slowly. But then you are aware that readers—any kind readers who've stayed with you—are bracing themselves for some revelation of sexual abuse. That's the usual horror. Mine is more diffuse. It wrapped a strangling hand around my life, and I don't know how to name it, I don't know what it was.

I am seven, seven going on eight. It is mid-morning of an ordinary day. I am in the yard at Brosscroft; I am playing near the house, near the back door. Something makes me look up: some shift of the light. My eyes are drawn to a spot beyond the yard, beyond its gate, a spot in the long garden. It is, let us say, some fifty yards away, among coarse grass, weeds, and bracken. I can't see anything, not exactly see: except the faintest movement, a ripple, a disturbance of the air. I can sense a spiral, a lazy buzzing swirl, like flies; but it is not flies. There is nothing to see. There is nothing to smell. There is nothing to hear. But its motion, its insolent shift, makes my stomach heave. I can sense—at the periphery, the limit of all my senses—the dimensions of the creature. It is as high as a child of two. Its depth is a foot, fifteen inches. The air stirs around it, invisibly. I am cold, and rinsed by nausea. I cannot move. I am shaking; as if pinned to the moment, I cannot wrench my gaze away. I am looking at a space occupied by nothing. It has no edges, no mass, no dimension, no shape except the formless; it moves. I beg it, stay away, stay away. Within the space of a thought it is inside me, and has set up a sick resonance within my bones and in all the cavities of my body.

I pluck my eyes away. It is like plucking them out of my head. Grace runs away from me, runs out of my body like liquid from a corpse. I move from the spot. My body weighs heavy, my feet have to be hauled up from the ground as if they were sticking in gore. I walk out of the sunlight, through the Glass Place, into the enclosed dimness of the cold kitchen. I say, Mum, I want to come in now, can I do some drawing?

I see myself through her eyes: sweat running from me, my cheeks fallen in, my chest heaving to control the thick taste of blood and sick that's in my mouth.

I pray, Let her not look at me.

Yes, she says, sweetly, her back turned. Of course you can.

It is the best yes I have ever heard. It is the best yes I have ever heard in the course of my life. If I had been sent out again, into the secret garden, think I would have died: I think my heart would have stopped.

This is the beginning of shame. I can feel it beginning in my life, tick-tick-tick, shame the timekeeper; a sick oscillation in the blood. My first thought is that I have seen the devil, that he did not wholly intend to show himself, and that I have only seen him because of a careless mistake on his part. I know that if you observe other people's mistakes—and they know you have observed them—they will make you suffer for it.

For I imagine the devil, when he goes to walk in the world, spruces himself in his dressing room, where the fire burns blue in its grate and the mirrors are draped with black. I imagine how he sleeks his rough fur with babies' fat, polishes his teeth with ground bones, and swills his mouth with blood; then taking from its peg his tall shiny hat, he sets it upon his head to hide his horns. Its riband is trimmed with plucked feathers from the wings of screaming angels that he chuckles over each day, moribund cherubs who he tickles with a scaly finger as he inspects his toothed steel traps. He pauses on the threshold, patting for his wallet, checking his pockets for his whips and stings. Anxious for respectability, he pulls kid gloves over his claws, but the claws split them. He squints up at God's sky, shakes out his umbrella of skin, and closes behind him the doors of hell: trapping in its sulfur reek. Almost instantly he is transported to where he wishes to be. He stands on the moorland looking down at Hadfield, his split hooves gleaming, his bestial profile blurred and smirking by the wet hazy light of the moon.

My grandmother had told me that if I made faces at myself in the mirror of her sideboard the devil would arise and stand behind my shoulder. I had tested this many times and found it not to be true. So what had occurred seemed to me a sort of slippage of diabolic etiquette; I had caught the devil betwixt and between. In our nightmares the devil is almost solid, his gaseous potbelly jutting, his opera cloak rippling behind him into the murk. Then he dissolves, fading into our flesh as we wake, just as the Communion Host fades into our teeth and tongue; Lucifer becomes a murmur, a heart murmur, a bubble in the blood. He tempts us to disobedience, to talking back and contradicting, to showing a will of our own; also to those violent and hateful sins found at the back of the catechism, such as murder, sodomy, oppression of the poor, and depriving laborers of their wages. Worse than these, more proximate to me, are the vices of blasphemy and inflicting brain damage. Brain damage would occur for sure if you were to drop a baby, or permit any injury to his skull. You are careful not to do this, you place your curving palm always over the fluffy crown of hair, over the place where the bones are closing. But what if the devil came behind you and whistled sharply, if he startled you and made you lose your grip, so the shocked baby shot from your arms like a greased pig, so he plummeted to the stone flags? You think about it, and push the thought away, thrusting it into a mental drawer and banging the drawer shut. But next the devil tempts you to blasphemy, he lurks on a Sunday morning in the shape of the Protestant child next door; he offers you to eat chewing gum before taking Communion, so God's body will be entangled in its strings.

You have not done these things. You have held tight the baby and declined the chewing gum. So far you are morally in the clear. But now you have committed a vice not mentioned in any catechism you know. You have managed to be in the wrong place at the wrong time, and so you have seen what no human person was meant to see.

I asked myself, was it an excuse, that you were too scared to move? I answered myself: there was no excuse. This creature didn't live—I reasoned it slowly—in the world of excuses. It was no use to say, I couldn't help seeing it. The fact was, *I should not have been looking*. Good children up and down the street—let's say stout Bernadette, let's say the two Margarets, one stout and blond and good at sums, one stoop-shouldered and blushing—they weren't messed around by this sort of apparition—only me, me in my family, me in my family when I'm seven going on eight, me in my family when I have reached the age of reason. There is a discipline enjoined on nuns, called "custody of the eyes." It means, for God's sake don't gawp about you. Look where you need to look, and nowhere else. But I had failed to keep my gaze under command. By a careless act I had gawped down the garden. Then hadn't I stared, fascinated, hypnotized, at what was happening; given it credence, before I'd even given it a name?

I was aware of this: to look for one second condemns you. There was some space of time—a tenth, twentieth, thirtieth of a second—in which you should have pulled your head away. You can bleach your eyeballs now or blind yourself, but you can't wipe out what you've seen. I imagine the iris scrubbed away, blue running into white, so that when you look into my eyes they are blank, gray-white and blind, like the canvas in a boxing ring.

In the days afterward I walked over the site of the disaster. The garden was still half-wild like a field, the grass rough and growing in tussocks. There was no mark on the ground, no scorched or bare patch; I did not think there would be, though I was aware that, if I were younger or medieval, I might have expected it. There was nothing to distinguish that undistinguished place, and yet I could put my hand on your arm and take you there; come with me, say your prayers now, I will take you to that very place. Was I afraid when I walked the ground? Not really; or, no more than usual. Outside was inside, now. Wherever I was, home or school, night or day and in bed or abroad, what I'd seen accompanied me. When sick old people wheeze, you might think there's a cat in the room, purring under the bedclothes; but the noise is generated in the cavity of the chest. In the same way, I cannot separate myself from what I have seen. I can't say, "There's it and there's me": it *is* me. It is part of me, like the innocent whorls of my fingerprints, or my ignorant hair growing from its roots; it is a body inside my body, an amphibian shape, budding and malign.

After this event, I am always more or less ashamed and afraid. At nine, I find myself blushing violently, and my head turning away as if my neck had become subject to a torsion, a nervous estrangement from the soldierly business of eyes front. I have ceased to confide in my grandfather. It is my brothers who sit on his knees and hear the tale of Giant Gazonka, and of how their ancestor became a sanitary inspector: how the villain

Murphy led the mob, wielding his wire whip. Myself I have shiny black shoes with the heels raised a fraction, as if a woman's shoes have pupped. I have lipstick put on, if my mother is in the mood for it, and a pink X of lipstick on my cheeks; the X rubbed in with her fingertips, so that I wear a consumptive's flush. Just playing! she says. You can't have makeup every time you go out! By now a puffy swelling has begun around my nipples, and I experience a queasiness, the ghost of the nausea that beset me in the secret garden. Sometimes without warning a pain grips around my navel, like the apprentice studding of a claw. When I feel it I double over, protecting the soft parts of me. Jack says, she's got colic, Mum, I can tell, I used to have colic something chronic. His voice is boyish, a London voice which breaks sometimes, partway through a sentence. Let her stay home, Mum, he says.

I stay home ("At home," I say carefully to myself. I won't be changing my syntax for Jack). I read to the little boys and make string harnesses for imaginary horses. Girls at school are mad on horses now but I could ride before I could walk. They are mad on ballet even though it's not Catholic. I find somewhere a catechism that is even older than the ones we use in school. The school ones have a blue paper cover but this one is fatter and covered in paper the color of a ginger biscuit. It has extra sections at the back describing advanced sins. The sins against the Holy Ghost are presumption and despair. I read it at night when I am in bed, until the summer daylight fails, and dies back over the moorland and the fields. In the dark I hold it, and sometimes write in it, very faintly in pencil, my comments and queries. Its back is falling off, owing to the advanced piety of the person who handled it before me.

Picture me now, more than thirty years later, sitting in a doctor's public waiting room: a place which, to me by then, approximates an antechamber of hell. My hands are clasped; I am not praying, I am wringing them. I stare about me at my fellow patients, slouching or fidgeting on hard molded chairs ranged around the room. They are pawing the public magazines left out for their diversion, disintegrating rags about celebrity weddings, engagements, divorces; they cough wetly over the full-color picture spreads of the happy or unhappy pair. How can they read, I think, or even flick through, scuffling and rifling through the pages? How can they goggle at those pictures, are they not sick with fright, do they not apprehend what sort of place this is?

Good God, says my new doctor, is that your pulse? Ah well, I say, I've just run up your stairs. He waves me to a seat, lets me be, tries it again. It's, you know, shall we say, perhaps, an artefact, I say, because I'm here in this situation, I'm not my usual self—but the more I smile and flutter and try to divert him, the more my heart's pounding. Then I tell him, by way of charming him, how when we learned First Aid as girls of fifteen I never learned any, because I was always the patient. I was the lightest to carry, always the one stretchered and bandaged, always the one whose fast pulse was hard to count. But it's just me, I plead. It's my constitution. Heart races, breathing shallow. Does it do any harm? He looks at me, he makes a note. He says gravely, book a double appointment, as soon as you feel able. I shall begin to examine you. I shall only begin. I will stop if you feel afraid.

I had thought, the heart's a muscle. It's Friday's child: Friday's child works hard for a living. Its speed I took for granted, its speed made me run; fear ran in my bloodstream, a seething soup in which my rational thoughts bobbed like dumplings. I thought it was a precondition of living; since the time of the secret garden I had thought that you were obliged to go on and on pitching yourself into battle and working up your level of panic, and that the moment when you stopped being frightened was the moment you knew you were dead. I was frightened to leave my grandfather—what young soldier would not be? I was frightened of Jack, with his brown masculine body always on show, lifting weights in the Glass Place: his pumped-up biceps and his fuzz of chest hair and the androgenic whiff that escaped from the clotted pillow of hair under his arms. I was afraid for my father, Henry, with his humble body so white, his Aertex vest drooping from his shoulders as he quickly and modestly undressed, turning away from me—his daughter and room-mate—so that I could not see his male organ. I thought I had seen it; but I imagined it to be like the coy, pointed organs of my little brothers, which the elder of them prettily indicated and called "my tail." I was afraid for my mother, who did not go out of the house much; but this did not save her, for one day the woman next door came berating her, hurtling from her kitchen and flying at the fence.

The sun was shining; it was a rare thing, but I remember some dazzling summers as the 1960s came in. Jack walked around in swimming trunks; he tanned easily. He did exercises and lifted weights; the muscles that strapped his ribs and belly were like ropes pulled tight beneath his skin. You did not need to be in sight of him to know he was weight lifting; you could hear the rattle as the big discs bumped into the small. He lifted in the yard, when the sun shone; in the kitchen, if the weather was inclement, laying down his wooden bench between the sink and the table. He wiped the sweat off his hands, to get (he explained) a good grip on the bar. He lay on his back and I heard his work-up pant, *ah-a, ah-a*: then the deep preparatory breath, his fingers locking on the metal, *oof-oo, oof-oo, aaa-agh!* He straightens his brown arms: the bar is in the air. Oh, look, look! says my mum; are you looking, boys? *Ah, ah,* his breath comes short: he blinks, sweat jumps from his brow, his breath lengthens, *wheef-ah, wheef-ah;* the trembling of the muscles: then *aha, aha,* the collapse of the weights, *whoof!* He drops them so hard that when they hit the floor they bounce; again you hear that flat metallic chink, like temple bells.

I preferred to be somewhere else when he lifted weights; in another room or, failing that, with my back turned. I used to think the bar might collapse and crush his voice box; that would stop his shouting. Jack's skull looked frail, as if his intelligence were bulging out of the skin at his temples. A pulse flickered there and beat; his brown eyelids rippled with thin gray-blue veins. Weights could kill him, I thought, but I did not hope for this because my mother said Jack put the bread in our mouths. When he rose from his bench his chest was thrust out, the sun catching its hair and making it into a nest of writhing wire; he turned away, and his thin yellow bottom shrank away from the edge of his trunks. Jack wrote articles for a magazine on physical culture. The magazine's name was *Health & Strength*. My mother said they paid up to a guinea for suitable material. One article was accepted! The editor sent him a congratulatory letter. "Yours, Oscar," it said.

So on this day of the neighbor attack, my mother lay on the grass, her sun-colored hair flickering as if she made, by herself, the temperature shoot up. Without warning, our neighbor was upon us, her jaw wide open and emitting shrieks and her tiny biceps jumping, as she gripped the fence, beneath the chicken skin of her dead-white arms: *you* there with your fancy man in the garden in the bright light of day and this a Saturday, canoodling with him *you* in nothing but your floral swimming costume and showing your very thighs, showing your skin and your very children, *your* children, *my* children, that *my* children should have to see the spectacle—my mother cut her short.

She rose from where she was basking, blinked, then turned and dawdled indoors, moving with indolent slowness, as if, slightly annoyed by a fly, she was going for the insect spray. Her floral shape flickered and darkened behind the panes of the Glass Place, till she passed through the kitchen door, which was standing open, and was swallowed by the darkness of the house itself. The woman rocking on the fence continued to spit and gibber, because she had primed herself, she had primed herself to her full tirade, she did not know how to abort it. Even as my mother was vanishing, she turned her head back over her shoulder, and saw *me;* as her green almond-shaped eyes flicked like darting fish, she saw me standing four-square, my hands on my hips, planted and staring at this object, this scrawny disgrace, this apology for a woman, this *Protestant,* whose tongue-lashing was as feeble as the lashing of the tail of a well-stamped scorpion.

When I came inside, dusting off my hands—literally I am sure, and not metaphorically—my mother said, thoughtfully, "You did that very well." I had developed my shield against Hadfield, the human shield of my flesh; I had developed the requisite indifference to public opinion, but—what was even more important—the snarling willingness for a public brawl. Was it that day, there and then, that my mother made up her mind to get us out? So that I didn't have to use those weapons, didn't have to waste my youthful ingenuity working up insults for the next standoff? I thought of the men who went out to fight, Saturday night, tottering into the gutter punctured and drunk, and of the sisters and wives who wiped the vomit off their chins and hauled them home, pocketing their smashed teeth for souvenirs.

Your life can go by in brooding; or your mind swerve violently, onto some other course. I did not need to think every day
of what had happened in the garden, of the neighbor attack or
the day of the devil; the buzz was in my bones. I thought of the
Satan I'd seen, caught unprepared, caught napping, waking
and stretching in his rank grassy bed before noon; sitting up
slowly and looking about him, rubbing his eyes with his hairy
forepaws so that the spores of anthrax fell out. How the devil
did I get here? the devil says, yawning, blinking, scratching his
belly. Is this Hadfield? More than likely. Have I been here
before? Certainly yes. Oh me, oh my. Is this where I'm dancing
tonight? Devil stretches, devil flexes, devil hums a tune; and
caught, transfixed, I listen, sickness rising inside me. He's step-
ping out to breathe an atmosphere that simply reeks of class.
His ebony cane in his claw, he's going to hot-hoof over the
ridge tiles of Bankbottom and up to Brosscroft, tippy-tap on
the slates. He takes in his stride the sects, our similar houses,
some with a picture of the pope and some not; some with
pianos, all with their humble puffing chimney and shack for
coal, their worn linoleum and threadbare towels hanging on a
nail by the kitchen sink. He sees us washing, he sees us eating,
he sees us lacing our shoes; he envies us our pink cake of soap,
our dish of tripe, our heels, and our soles. He envies the sta-
tionmaster blowing his whistle, the green electric train on its
track; he envies that track. Over the roofs of our rival churches
he flies, downhill to St. Andrews and uphill to St. Charles; he
hovers over their downspouts and guttering, and strips their
lead with his passing teeth.

When I think of it, that casual yet purposive buzz of Satan
waking up, I see again his clothes brush clutched in his antici-
patory hand, and his tarry shoe polish compounded of livers
and spleens, and his patent pumps that hide his evil trotters. I

see him buffing his fore claws, studding his collar with calcined eyeballs; for he's putting on his top hat, putting on his white tie, putting on his tails.

In the years ahead I was always cold when I woke up, and (because my mother regulated the household by her own fierce need to keep thin) I was often vaguely hungry. I decided to ignore the signals the body sends; when I listened to my mind, there was only an echo chamber that sent back a feeble reiteration of the world at work around me. At eleven, twelve, I took long walks, meaning to notice nature; nature noticed me. I seemed to have small capacity for abstract reasoning. I could find the area of a field or calculate compound interest, and I could perform feats of trigonometry provided I didn't read the tables of logarithms backward, provided I didn't have to think about the meaning of what I was doing. But when Jack tried to teach me algebra I would shrink away, trying to melt my spine into the chair back, trying to buckle into the wood. My eyes blurred. My hunger would turn to a sharp pain, then sickness. You hate me, I would be thinking, looking at the tired, harassed man beside me. Why pretend you don't? You don't want to teach me algebra. You want to erase me. You want to start again with my mother and the pliant little boys who stagger after you, calling, "Jack . . . Jack . . . oh, Jack, can we screwdriver, can we hammer, ple-ease can we lift your weights?"

"You see," he would say, "Ilary . . .": tiny pearls of sweat would dance on his forehead. He'd have ended his working day snarling and sweating through the evening traffic. I myself, worn out from the day's enforced sociability, from the perils of friends and enemies, from hauling my leather bag of books home through the autumn fogs, would want nothing more than a moment in which to recollect myself, to study an irregular verb or two and learn a verse. But my mother knew it was

Wednesday, black Wednesday, algebra night. I could hear her voice carrying down the hall (this was another house, not Brosscroft): "I never had the *opportunity of algebra*. Let alone anyone who could teach it to me."

An hour would pass, Jack's breathing becoming more and more like that of a man who is lifting weights; my hands would be shaking. Jack and my mother—the couple who had endured, to be together, so much adverse public opinion—had run away to live in shady coupledom, pretending to be married but without the due certification. They were living a life as puzzling to me as—let Mrs. Malaprop say it—an allegory on the banks of the Nile. Jack had been in the army, in Egypt like my grandad. He never told of the zoo at Cairo, or of startling meetings with future world leaders; aggressively, he denied history, personal or collective. I agree with Henry Ford, he said: history is bunk. He wielded his proverb against me, when history drew me in, history with its weighty aggregations of fact. Before we left Hadfield my mother had made an effort, out of her small budget, to buy me a child's periodical called *Look and Learn*. I was nine and a half, I was ten, I looked, I learned; sometimes I found inconsistencies in what I read. Which to believe, my library book, or *Look and Learn*? Who invented the telephone: Alexander or Graham Bell? Sometimes I captured the smaller Margaret, the blushing one, Margaret also known as Walter. I asked her angrily what she believed, the first thing she was told or the second? I took her by the wrist, by the cuff of her white school blouse, and harangued her; what was her policy in the matter? For what did these letters stand, USSR? My mother said it was the United States of Soviet Russia. Later evidence suggested different. Could she give me her most recent take on these initials?

Margaret stretched her eyes, she pulled away, her cheeks

flamed scarlet; she looked as if she might be sick. I felt for her. Nothing is more shameful than avoidable error.

All that was preserved of Jack's life in Egypt was preserved in a handful of scrappy photographs. Group poses were unkind to the English men of the 1950s; stand a few of them together, and they look like a welfare line. In uniform or out, they are malnourished scraps, their hair sheared with clippers and their ears sticking out, their expressions anxious, temporary: they seem always on their way from somewhere to somewhere, carrying their old dad's kit bag and wearing his trousers.

The photographs are small, white-edged, blurred. Jack's mates, off duty, pose outside a military hut of some kind, a temporary building in a waste of light. They have taken their shirts off; the white racks of their ribs like those of animals disdained at market. Their mouths are open in snaggle-toothed smiles, and they hold between them a life-size cutout photo of Marilyn Monroe. She looks twice their bulk, dead-eyed and puffy, her bottom lip shining like a peeled snake. They wear a group expression of simulated lechery; their wrists and bony phalanges wrap about her thighs.

Does this photo come in the post, courtesy of some nostalgia freak? It's too much for my mother, though Jack's own hands are well away from the cardboard date with her lofted breasts. When my mother sees Marilyn she tosses her chin up, narrows her eyes; she makes a sound of disgust, tongue against hard palate; she walks out of the room. She is beautiful; therefore no one else can be.

Sergeant Foster, my grandfather, had been photographed in Cairo in 1919. It was a studio shot, uniformed; he had taken off his cap and rested it behind him on a tall stand placed for the purpose, his Machine Gun Corps badge aligned for the camera. He was seated on a cane chair, his eyes bright and his mouth unsmiling beneath his small, sleek mustache. Many years later, in some railway bivouac, some late-night crossover point where crews waited to retrain, he heard a man his own age talking about his war; of how one day, the worst day of his life, he had been trapped, pinned down along with his troop, of how he had thought in his desperation that they were all dead meat. But then some shrewd sergeant saw their plight, gave them covering fire, gave them a slit of opportunity to swarm through, and they took it. "It is thanks to that man I'm alive," he said. "I have been told he was known as Judd Foster: that he came home alive also, and is employed on the railways now. And it is my ambition to shake that man's hand."

It is strange that, though this story awed me, I don't know the end of it. Did my grandfather lean across the room—the room half-lit, half-heated, by a flickering paraffin stove—did he lean out of the shadows, offering his hand? If so, why did nothing ensue, no exchange of mementos, letters? Why is there no picture of the salvaged comrade, his name traced on the back in spidery copperplate, and why is there no family story to go with him? I imagine this night, the huddle of men, the railwaymen, their faces turned to the storyteller, their different badges of authority and rank, their silver buttons gleaming against the coarse near-black of their uniforms; some with their lives before them, some with their best years gone. Had he seen too much, the sergeant-instructor, was the time for shake-hands lost? He rose, I believe, from his bench at the back, and walked out unremarked onto the platform, looking up and down the track for the distant wink from the signals, red or green. England was dark in those days, its acres unpopulated, its nights full of the breathing of animals and the eyes of its dead shining from hedgerows and copses. He fumbled for a cigarette and lit it, holding it close in crooked finger-joints, turned into the cup of his hand as the men of his generation did; the soldier after dusk does not show a light. Crisscrossing the points the trains run of themselves, unmonitored by the eye of God, the junctions and the marshaling yards, the crossings and the unmanned halts, their dull tracks the veins and arteries of the nation. The time for war stories has passed; years have gone by and we have dwindled into civilians. Men who war had broken were all around him, Annie Connor's husband coming back with his leg lost, his fierce temper alternating with silences, silences prolonged for weeks; Joe O'Shea, his wife's brother, health broken in the military prison, his babies dead of pneumonia, that cold viral wind that blows down the years. Dead Englishmen and Irishmen, called to the service of king and country; is this not the country, this mesh flung over the uplands and river valleys, this net of metal which holds it safe, marked out in points of light? I see him raise his head, look down the track, narrow his eyes, and exhale; his breath drifts out to join the night, the long blue night of the obscure.

In the years after the apparition in the garden, I didn't talk about it much—never, until I was secure in my trade or profession as writer—aware that if I did so I would be questioned, invited to make an analysis, and that any analysis I might make would cut against its phenomenological truth. Sometimes I would laugh and say, I'm like Aunt Ada Doom, I saw something nasty in the woodshed. I say that, like Ada of Cold Comfort Farm, I was never the same afterward, seven going on eight was the point when my sweet nature curdled, and I ceased to expect much good from the world after that.

I know this is true and a half-truth. When people ask what is the nature of evil, I should like to stand up and say, I can contribute an anecdote. But what my anecdote means, I don't know. I am left uncertain, with evidence that I can't add up. Is evil simply—simply?—an outgrowth of human nature, or is it detachable from the human, a force at large in the world like a mercenary for hire, looking for a human master to serve, never without one for long and always worth the whistle? I think of the garden, the broad daylight, the slow-moving sinister aggregation of cells, and ask myself if it was something never seen in nature, like a cancer looking for a host. How long would it last without human attention?

I read about a company of actors staging Marlowe's *Dr. Faustus*, who counted among the masked players onstage one extra, a player they did not know; how they ran from the stage screaming, and the audience in panic scattered too. I would like to write their story or make a film of it, but life is not long enough for all the intelligent variations on all the narratives of fear.

I can talk about the secret garden now and do it in different modes, comic or tragic or satiric. I can write about it, but say twenty drafts are not good enough, suppose the publisher is e-mailing to say he wonders when I'll be through? Then I lurch out into a new version, comic probably, some new version sprightly and defended; but recovering, each time some fresh sickening detail. When I'm on my own, and I think about it privately, then I scarcely laugh at all.

Let me go back a little. I pick up my life, six months or so after the devil; I am eight. Annie Connor dies. Not so suddenly; her chest heaves and wheezes, she takes to her bed. Though I see them at dinnertime, my grandad and grandma and Aunt Annie, I would not dream of failing to call on them as I come home from school, to have a cup of tea and a bun. One afternoon I am taken up the stairs at no. 58, and as soon as I see Annie I know by the leaden, pooled blood in the veins of her face that she is dying.

I toil up the hill to Brosscroft. My mother sometimes watches for me. Just as I can't hear a straight sentence when it's spoken, I can't walk a straight line: she knows that the merest dot in the distance is me, if it is weaving around the pavement.

My mother's eyes scour my face. She doesn't want to be tempted down the hill to Bankbottom, if this is a false alarm; old aunts cough and wheeze, it's what they do. "Do you think she is dying?" my mother says.

She looks into my eyes: as on the night when I told her not to switch on the gas. For the second time, she credits me with sense. She shoots down the hill. I am not with her, so I don't know what happens. But I know a kind of peace is made, between the households: or, less of a war.

It is a Saturday morning. My mother comes into my bedroom. I have my own room now, at the back of the house, papered by Jack in pink and white. My mother says, "Auntie Annie has gone to live with Jesus."

I turn my face away and cry. She means it for the best, but I think it was unnecessary to phrase it like that, as if I were a six year old. Adults want you to know things, then unknow them. But knowledge doesn't go backward. I would have understood a simple "dead," and I can't unsee her livid, mottled face. In a way, I tell myself, it is good to have seen a dying person, and recognized her state.

I turn to the back of my big ginger catechism and find a prayer which claims it never fails. I pray it. I want my Aunt Annie and I pray that she may come back.

I know God won't deliver. He won't deliver on that sort of prayer and what I'm doing by praying it is blaspheming: kicking his godly and his god-awful shins. He didn't help me in the secret garden, and I think he couldn't anyway; I think that whatever I saw that day was more powerful than any bewhiskered prayer-book God, simpering in a white robe: his holy palms held apart, as if He were sizing up a plank. Why didn't he try, though? He could have done something. He could have showed willing. I wanted him to manifest, and own me, take charge. But he never turned up, in the secret garden; the old bugger never got out of bed. Now, a graceless being, abandoned, I pray silly stuff to spite him. You have these so-called prayers that always work; on the other hand, you know that the past can't be recalled. Time doesn't flow backward; all the scientists say so.

Soon afterward, leaving school at twelve o'clock, I hurtle straight downhill, down the carriage drive and across the road. It is a main road, and the carriage drive comes out on a straight · run between two deep bends. But there is little traffic, none of it fast: who would need to speed toward Hadfield?

I escape by inches. I look back, to the long black car that has squealed to a halt; I shudder once, and bolt for home.

Big girls have turned back; they are screaming. They pounce on me, as I try to zigzag past them; I want to run up the road to Bankbottom, but they won't let me. I go rigid; they half-lift me and drag me back toward the scene of the incident, my heels scraping the ground. The driver has put his window down, and is leaning out of it. He is a man with a bald dome, sleek wings of hair at the sides of his head. My own head is ducked by a big girl's palm, and my face is thrust toward his; he wants to see me, they want to exhibit me. He is shaking. Did you not see me, he says? He is not angry, but guilty, aghast; he is a stranger. His fingers are curling around the wheel to control their quiver. Did you not see me? I pity him. There is cold sweat on his forehead, like the sweat of death.

I am tugging to be away. My child compeers are gathered—well, trust them to be in on a drama! Others are pouring down the drive, so are teachers and nuns. Two big girls have me by the wrists, and are trying to persuade me back up the drive to the school. In silence I pull away from them, teeth clenched. I pull, they pull, till I am in danger of being divided, like the child in the judgment of Solomon. They are fifteen years old, with great brawny arms, with the woody scent of motherhood rushing from their pores and enveloping me. I make a plot, I devise a ploy; I allow myself to be drawn forward, sweetly, then I spring into the air and hurl myself backward to the length of my arms. Their grips yield: I run. All I want to do is run: to 56 Bankbottom, to my grandma. Inside I'm howling with rage. I'm alive, what's the problem? What's new? I live and die by inches.

My grandma is giving me beans on toast. She sinks on one knee to toast the bread before the fire. I love this meal; but today it dries in my throat. I cannot swallow. Her puzzled face swims after me as I creep back to school for the afternoon.

Next day—it takes time for the news to reach her—comes the rant from Mrs. Stevens. I am shouted at and held up as an example of a person nearly dead, nearly dead by my own ignorant self-willed dashing. And what do they say at home, what do they have to say about it all, hm, hm? I sit in a sullen, snarling silence. My "best friend" Bernadette raises her hand and says, "Miss, she's not told 'em."

Not told 'em? What? Not carried home to my grandmother the news that I am just a foot or eighteen inches from being ground into the tarmacadam, my arms fluttering and my neck snapped like a pigeon's? A long "aw—hh" from the class is shouted down by Mrs. Stevens. Now I am accused of being a deceiver, as well as nearly dead. My "best friend" whispers that I'll have to tell it in Confession: it's worse than a lie, she says. And before the week is out, a distant relative, seldom seen, turns up at Bankbottom with a highly colored account of the occasion: the screech of tires, the burned rubber on the road, the cry of nuns, the preemptive tolling of church bells.

This is a child's life. You have no rights, over your life or death. Every event that happens to you is appropriated by others, who think they know better than you do what is going on in your head. So don't speak, even under threat, especially under threat; don't feed them information they can use against you. In the court of public opinion you're sentenced: toll the dead bell.

I have my own courtroom, my own trial. A noose for Mrs. Stevens. A noose for my distant relative. A noose for my "best friend." A noose for Mother Malachy, headmistress of my school, who stood at the gate, gloating over the drama, and propelled those great girls down the drive to tear me apart. But grace for the driver. Grace for the great girls. Grace for me, running; grace for my sealed lips; for my grandma, kneeling before the fire. Except there's no point in praying for grace or asking for it anymore, since God is obviously looking but not looking in my direction.

Now that Grandad was retired, he had more time for testing me on spellings. First every day he oversaw my dinner, indulging me—take that piece of the loaf, it is what you prefer. Let's see you eat this cake; this kind of cake is what we call a

Savoy. My sad and nauseous days gave him the more excuse for ingenuity, carving an apple into slices, and laying it out on a plate, tempting and sugared.

But a day came when he felt his age, and mine too, and then he led me up the steep stair to the garret, a room whistling with cold. There were white planks underfoot, and standing in the middle of the room, under the skylight, was a rabbit hutch. And in it were books.

Their pages were crisp and sallow, nibbled at the edges by time, or perhaps by rabbits. Their covers, once green, burgundy, and navy blue, now inclined to the condition of black, so ancient and tarry that I thought it would come off on my fingers: not that I gave a bugger, excuse me Father for swearing. I wanted books like a vampire wants blood. My daddy, Henry, took me to the Hadfield library, where there was one bookcase for children, and I had read it upside down and inside out. I had read the books so hard that when I gave them back the print was faint and gray with exhaustion, and I thought that one day the librarian would notice how I had been depleting them and tear my ticket up.

My own bedroom at Brosscroft was a room where the sun shone, the only room in the house in which you were safe to put anything down without it being sucked into phantomland. Such books as we had were dumped there. Some had come to Jack in the course of his life: a set of yarns called *Out with Romany,* country lore and country life. Looking into it made me ask, was Hadfield the country, or the town? It seemed to occupy some no-man's-land, some place not well-defined in any book. There were very few streets, but very few trees. There were no badgers, curlews, kestrels. There were starlings who settled, their group mind instructing them, with their private glamour which shone out when the sun lit their sequined wings. Scattering, startled, their beaks darting, they bobbed about like debutantes searching for the buffet; even the most hard-hearted women fed them, with crumbs ground from the heels of loaves.

I read *Romany;* I learned to love the hedgehog, and the ways of sneaky fox. I read the horrible, foxed, moldy volume of Tennyson, someone's Sunday School prize: Mariana in the moated grange. I read *Steps to Literature: Book Five.* It was a small book, its pages yellow and decaying, its greasy cover stamped with the word "Specimen." Look inside: the subtitle was "Readings on Europe." It was a book of extracts. I read them all.

"In a certain village in La Mancha, there lived not long ago one of those old-fashioned gentlemen. . . ."

"It is now sixteen or seventeen years since I saw the Queen of France, then the dauphiness, at Versailles. . . ."

"Once she did hold the gorgeous East in fee . . ."

"I have sat for hours at my window inhaling the sweetness of the garden, and musing on the chequered fortunes of those whose history is dimly shadowed out in the elegant memorials around . . ."

I am mad about this book. Like Washington Irving at the Alhambra, I issue forth at midnight to get it. I wake up before dawn to read its single scene from *Julius Caesar:* the scene where Antony pitches the mob against Brutus. The scene is prefaced by an extract from Plutarch, so I am keyed in on the story line. I like the story, all of it: the violence, the polemic. I wish I had written it myself. Brutus, of course, was in the right. Antony had the best use of words. Beware words; beware the slick. "If you have tears . . ." Beware the sentimental crowd.

So this, I think, is the *Complete Works of Shakespeare,* a thing which I have heard people mention. In my opinion, it deserves all the applause people heap on it. I learn the death of Caesar by heart. I murmur it, in times of stress, as the pious murmur the Rosary.

One day, my breath held, hurrying, I go down into the yellow room, my old bedroom shared with my father. I look in the drawer of the little cabinet beside his bed. There I find my book of tales of King Arthur, which has been missing for as long as I can remember. I am overjoyed. I fall back into the stories. I now like the ones I used to miss out. I like the Grail. I imagine how the knight lies rigid in his bed while the chalice, half hidden in its veils and airy wrappings, glides slowly across his field of vision. In the back bedroom of my grandmother's house at Bankbottom—my mother's old bedroom, an empty room where I am allowed to play—I have sometimes seen similar shadows, objects that are unnameable, that float and are not solid, objects through which the wall behind them can be glimpsed. They seem to me domestic things, plates and cups, bowls: as if they were echoes or shadows of the objects in daily use in the kitchen below. In time I realize that anything in this room can become translucent. I spend a great deal of time there, mostly alone, pursuing no particular game, just being. Sometimes my old friend Evelyn comes to play. We peddle backward on an old child's bicycle that leans by the wall. My grandmother labors up the stairs with our favorite meal of banana sandwiches. The room, when Evelyn is in it, is entirely solid.

Winter: it is dark by half past four, and the curtains are drawn in the front room at Brosscroft. The evening is silent; Jack has gone to nightschool; my father, Henry, is somewhere else, at the jazz club or the library. By the light of the low-slumbering fire the brothers are undressed, and taken upstairs to bed. Their clothes come off in three effortful tugs, from their shoes and socks upward. It is my task to pick up after them, to strip vest from T-shirt and turn the arms of their jerseys the right way out: then uncrease and smooth them, spread them out to life size, as if I were making little boys from wool. I shake out their tiny socks from their scattered shoes, line up the four shoes in pairs, then put everything tidily away in a deep drawer by the fireside. Sometimes when they have gone, I sit gently on their rocking horse, which is really a springing horse, which bounces on a metal frame; I am too old for this toy, and the thought that I might be seen riding it brings a blush to my cheeks.

I am nine; knight errantry is behind me, and my progress is complete, from hero to zero. I am going to become a woman, though I cannot imagine of what sort. A little girl, flat-chested, can't imagine her body will ever change. One day she becomes conscious of the brushing of her blouse against her skin. She puts her fingers there—I do—and feels enraged at the thought of what is to come. The whole process is beyond control. You have no choice in it. My body is getting the better of me, though people seem to feel I am responsible for what it does. Now I am worse than blushing Margaret; my small blood vessels are unstable, and if anyone speaks to me, if anyone looks at me, my shame thuds crimson into my face. I can't help this, and the more I try to help it the worse it goes; it seems to drive my mother and Jack into a frenzy of irritation.

I listen; above I hear ponderous footsteps, I know the boys are not in bed yet. Cautiously, I let out my breath; I let the horse spring, beneath me: I trot it for a quarter of a mile. My fingers brush its reins and bridle, most unconvincingly rendered in painted metal. I raise my eyes, and they rest on the drawn curtains of our front room at 20 Brosscroft. Against a background of silver gray, the curtains have a repeating design—of windows.

They are Mediterranean windows, with gay blinds and plants spilling from pots and wrought-iron baskets. I appraise them; my cold northern soul flips in my chest. I want to live behind those windows and to be warm. There are two patterns of window, one rectangular and one arched, and I can't choose between them; the rectangle is more elegant, the arch more enticing. At 20 Brosscroft, firelight gutters, drafts suck at the flames, the Glass Place rattles, the garden yields up its dead secrets. But at the Alhambra, as *Steps to Literature* assures me, "the garden beneath my window is gently lighted up, the orange and citron trees are tipped with silver, the fountains sparkle in the moonbeams, and even the blush of the rose is faintly visible." I imagine my life behind those windows, the texture of my life: I carry the sun inside me as I move through the shaded, scent-drenched rooms.

Many years later, I asked my mother if she remembered the Brosscroft curtains, the curtains with the window design. I used to imagine, I said, that I vanished into their texture and lived there, within the warp and weft of their cloth; that I lived behind their shutters and balconies, that I owned those window boxes and those pots with the spilling scarlet flowers. My mother turned away, so that I couldn't see her face. She whispered, and I, oh so did I.

Those were cold years for her. Love doesn't light the meager fire in the grate or fill the children's bellies. And childhood was a sort of gulag for me; I was cut off, adrift. Conditions changed from year to year; sometimes I moved to another camp, where I waited to see if the regime would be better or worse, more or less survivable, and where I scrambled quickly to learn the rules. It wasn't particularly anyone's fault. Few people acted with malice toward me. It was just that I was unsuited to being a child.

At ten, I developed catastrophic hay fever. I sneezed and shook for a whole summer long, my weeping eyes were blind and sealed to slits. Between my eyelids I saw flashes of scarlet, the petals of flowers: geraniums.

When the day of the Eleven Plus results came, I was at home as usual, sick. I had no expectation that I would earn a grammar school place, and no particular hope of it. It seemed out of my hands—as it had been for Grandad, whose parents couldn't afford the uniform: as it had been for my mother, whose teachers had simply forgotten to enter her for the exam.

Just after four o'clock Bernadette came to the door. I went to open it. She stood squarely on the front step and looked me up and down. "Ye've passed," she said, unsmiling.

I fell back into the house, my hands across my heart. And you?

Soberly, she nodded. Perhaps she was in shock.

"Give Bernadette some orange juice," my mother said.

I went into the dim pantry with the deep stone shelves. The ghosts rolled under them, sucking their teeth in envy and malice. My hand trembled, the neck of the bottle knocked against the rim of the glass. Passed. Who would have thought it? Passed. So I can have a life, I thought.

Within a few weeks we were moving house: myself, not my father, my mother, Jack, the two little brothers and the one dog that was left. By the end of the summer we would be gone. We would be gone to another town. We would have a semidetached house. It would have a lawn. It would have a rockery; it would have an apple tree, and "even the blush of the rose is faintly visible." We would have new carpets and another name.

We would be gone so fast that by September, when the new school year began, we would be a scorched trail on the air.

My childhood ended so, in the autumn of 1963; the past and the future equally obscured by the smoke from my mother's burning boats.

Smile

———

For the next seven years, I lived with my mother and Jack, two brothers and a dog, in a house in a small town in Cheshire.

Sometimes, when I had known Jack at first, he would lend me his fountain pen. The pen's name was written on its barrel: Swann. When I wielded Swann, my writing came out mysteriously like his, black and small and without ornament: a man's hand. But by the time I reached my teenage years, this privilege was withdrawn. I had to hack my own words onto paper with whatever deficient instrument came to hand. My handwriting was always changing, getting remodeled; my practical skills were not many, and those I had were hardly commercial. By the time he was midway through his teens, my brother who had kicked the bottom out of his pram could rip an engine out of a car, and practically build a house; at the same age I couldn't even wire a plug. I lived in terror that Jack would one day teach me how; but he didn't seem to think that women and electricity could be trusted together. Luckily for me, we had moved to a house where there was no gas.

• • •

When you go to a new country, or join a new tribe, the first thing you must learn is the ceremonies of greeting and farewell. In our new town—or "village," as it called itself, looking back steadfastly to the genteel past—the easy familiarities of Hadfield were nowhere in evidence. No one went from house to house with the gossip, or barged into your front room yelling, "It's me." People had bells on their doors, and those bells were for use. When people asked, "And how are you?" it was not a question that demanded a reply. When you left a shop, instead of Hadfield's downbeat "t'rah," they sang out, "Bye now!" Even men sang it; it didn't sound very manly. In Hadfield, men had no form of farewell that I could remember. If they were going out, why should they mention it? It wasn't your business. They simply wrenched open the door and hurled themselves, teeth gritted, into the moorland wind.

Our new house was on an avenue, not a street. It had a glass porch and a bay window, a hall, two rooms, a small poky kitchen: upstairs, two good bedrooms and a box room— mine—and a bathroom. A bathroom! Before we moved in we used to visit the house, for fixing-up sessions. The empty rooms smelled of floorboards. The little boys played in the garden, among the late summer ghosts of the hybrid teas. Secretly, upstairs by myself, I climbed into the bath without any water, with my clothes and shoes on, to see what kind of enclosure it was: where your head came, and where your feet. "It seems strange," I said to my mother dreamily, "to say you've never had a bath before." She looked at me in shrinking horror, as if she feared I might say that outside the house.

The bathroom was old-fashioned, and the first thing Jack did was to box the bath in so that you could not see its legs.

Later he made the paneled doors flush; everything was being squared up, modernized. My mother fixed a panel of black quilted plastic to the back of the sitting-room door, and secured it with shiny brass tacks. It was *le dernier cri*. None of the neighbors had such ideas about décor. Their houses, glimpsed but seldom entered, had patterned carpets and chintz; their pale wallpaper had flowers on, and there were lace mats on their sideboards. My mother was too go-ahead for a sideboard.

But there were some markers of the middle classes we could not do without. We went out to buy a three-piece suite. It was boxy and angular, moss-green with seat cushions of a dashing bold check; it was nothing like the suites of the neighbors. And those curtains that came only to the windowsill, my mother said, she powerfully despised. Our curtains with the windows on were left behind at Brosscroft; our new curtains had dramatic silk stripes and fell to the carpet. When they were drawn, shutting out the autumnal garden, the scrubby lawn littered with windfalls, the creaking pergola arch with the rotting wood and the rambling rose, I whispered to my mother, "It's like a stage." She smiled, gratified. Behind the curtains night fell, peaceful on ornamental stonework, on dwarf conifers and garden ponds; the drama was played out among us, the audience. Our house was like a million other houses in a million other streets, but our perplexities, our hesitations were all our own; we had secrets, and we did not think other households harbored any.

But I must have begun to know that every house was different, that every house had a secret life, because at the end of the summer of '63, after we moved into the avenue, I got into the habit of walking up and down, examining the façades of our neighbors, eyeing up their paintwork, and scrutinizing their shrubs. Then I went farther afield, up the avenues, drives, and closes, and around the crescents, noting how some houses had square bays and some had portholes for porch windows, some had panes of stained glass and some had scrolly metalwork gates instead of plain wood. Some houses had names. Ours was called "Arcadia." But the name had dropped off long ago, and it had become plain Number Four.

One day, a week or so before we moved in, I walked into an empty room and saw Jack's tweed jacket hanging from the doorknob. It surprised me; empty clothes have always been worrying to me, and it was as if Jack himself, being occupied elsewhere, had left the coat in loco parentis, imbued with his authority and power. The boys were outside, my mother and Jack were upstairs; I was alone. Sunshine spilled in at the uncurtained window. It was afternoon: that time, around three o'clock, when a day seems to pause and yawn, before stretching itself and ambling forward toward teatime. It was August; the air was still; there was no noise, from garden or street, neither car engine nor birdsong. I walked across to the jacket; I watched it for a moment, then touched its rough tweed. I stood for a time, my fingertips brushing it lightly. Then I put my face into it and breathed in the complex scents that collected in those days in fabrics: industrial smells of metal and rubber, rural smells of ordure and woodsmoke: the smoke of other people's cigarettes, the Cheshire smell of grass clippings, the lingering Derbyshire smell of peat. I felt a spasm of grief, as if Jack were dead, and as if his soul had gone into the weave of the cloth.

My grief may have been self-serving. Must have been, really. He was all we had now for a husband and a father, even though he was neither of these, and my mother didn't cease to remind me that not many men would have done what he did, take a family on. But why did she say this? It didn't make sense to me. I was determined not to be grateful for what was simply inevitable; it was like thanking somebody for the fact that it's Friday, or complimenting them on having a nose on their face. How could Jack have got her, without us? It wasn't possible. It wouldn't have worked. My mother was a jewel and her sons were her setting; I was her packaging material, to be ripped through in excitement and tossed away. So I felt. The boys could grow up and be Jack's, or as good as: men want sons. Nobody wants a skinny ten-year-old girl with sticky-out teeth and a habit of flinching when you speak to her: a girl who will soon be bleeding all over the bathroom at monthly intervals, whose stockings will always be laddered and whose fingers will always be inky, a thing not childlike, not womanly, always remembering, always knowing things.

When I went to my convent school at first I didn't know much. My last years at primary school had been conducted under the eye of Mother Malachy, which had rolled at me around the curve of her starched headdress. Many a dreary afternoon I would contemplate her, as she stood at the head of the class and prosed on about this or that. I studied her so that, when I was out of her presence, I could draw her, commit her to paper: my eye traced the bulb of her nose, the coarse swag of her chin. They were long, those days, those schooldays, and Malachy was a heavy static presence within them, her profile unyielding against the cold rainy light. At eleven years old, I knew, you failed your scholarship exam and moved on, to a new school for Catholic failures that had been built in Glossop; until recently, the failures had stayed at St. Charles and rotted, under Malachy's rule, until they reached the school-leaving age.

I thought I would never attain this failure; the days stretched themselves out, arithmetic in the morning out of the brown book, then a subject called Intelligence, then English out of the green book. *General Progress Papers,* the books were called, and they had gaps to fill in, where, with a blunt failing pencil, you tried to impose your version over the wrong answers of the people who had gone before, battling away against all the years of folly and error which—if you turned up the page and fingered the back of it—you could read like braille. I thought that time had stopped for me; I thought I should never be free of Malachy, never reach the age of eleven; I felt that she had absorbed me, drawn me to her by my woolly cardigan, by means of static electricity: drawn me into the fusty depth of her habit, and then leached me into her thick body, as if she were my mother indeed, and I was beating at the walls of her nunly womb. The lights burned all day in Hadfield winters, the great radiators puffed and fumed and stank, the odor of Wellington boots and nit lotion and nun became so thick you felt you could graze it with your knuckles; you were, very often, spoiling for a fight.

Malachy's idea of education was to use up a whole half hour by going around the class, asking the same daft question. In Lent, she said, the statues in church are draped with cloths, velvet cloths of purple black: did we all know that? Yes, Mother Malachy, we chorused: well, they did, I never chorused anything. So, she said to each child, how do you know that? After a prolonged, nervous hesitation—Mother Malachy was very violent—the first child had a happy inspiration. "My mother told me, Mother Malachy." Next child: "My mother told me, Mother Malachy." Halfway through—we'd have been, I suppose, thirty-five in the class—some exasperated hero broke out, "I remember it from last year, Mother Malachy." Shock rippled through the room. The rhythm was broken. But after another excruciating hesitation, the next child resumed, "My mother told me, Mother Malachy."

But when my turn came, I said nothing. Not a word would I yield. I had made a policy: I would answer reasonable questions, but not ones I thought were senseless. I would write the answer to any question, but speaking was different. Talking was forbidden to pupils in class. If the rule of silence had been imposed, I too could employ silence. Why should I speak because an arbitrary decision had been made, that it was the time for speech?

"Intransigence" was not a word I knew. But I was learning from my mother, learning to keep intact my own opinion of myself. I was learning it too early, though, for my circumstances. My adult reasoning and my small status were at odds. One day Mother Malachy hit me so hard in the face that she propelled me across the room, and spun around my head on the stalk of my neck. Ho, fisticuffs, Madam! I said to myself. I put a smile on my face and turned my head the right way round again. I'd seen her hand coming, sweeping up through her blurring draperies; I watched the boxing on TV with my father, Henry, and I knew how to move defensively, my feet were quick and my eyes also. I was eight then: blinking back the automatic tears that arise in response to a blow, in case they would be seen by her as a vindication. By the time I was ten, my contempt for her was so complete that I must have worn it like armor, for she never exerted herself to lay a finger on me. I was amazed, of course, when Bernadette came to the house, four o'clock on a spring afternoon, to tell me that we weren't going to Glossop to the school for Catholic failures; that we had passed our examination and were going, instead, to the Convent of the Nativity. I was still more amazed when I got there, and found that the nuns didn't punch you; not even the lay teachers seemed to want to go ten rounds with a six-stone opponent.

My convent school was a small, gentle institution, a little bit snobbish. Because it was considered the "good" school of the area, the Protestant burgesses of the district paid fees for their daughters to go there, in the knowledge that their girls would be turned out well-spoken, polite, and poised. The sheer numbers of Protestants per class shielded us from the worst excesses of religious zeal. Convent girls, of course, like to consider themselves as restricted, trammeled, and oppressed. So the actual conditions prevailing—which I thought quite liberal—did not prevent the girls telling each other in tones of shocked mirth those stories that are always current in convent schools: that Sister So-and-So had said—"to my elder sister," or "ten years ago"—that the Holy Virgin would never have sat on a boy's knee without putting a telephone directory under her thighs, or that Our Mother Mary would never have worn patent leather shoes in case they reflected her knickers. Mother Mary need not have troubled about the footwear; you would have seen nothing even if we'd walked over mirrors, because our maiden crotches were hugged tight by navy blue garments so thick and dense that they could with profit have been worn by men off to the Antarctic. My first set of knickers self-destructed in the course of time; how can this be, were they carried off by giant crows, or did someone throw acid on them as they hung on the washing line? I never got any new ones, so I was forced to rummage in our airing cupboard for whatever was around by way of shrunken nylon panties; and so for many years, and even when in course of time I was elected Head Girl, I slunk around with an illicit bottom.

The Convent of the Nativity, at first, had been off-limits to Hadfield girls, to Derbyshire girls in general. Any girl who sneaked under the wire and wasn't a Catholic failure was expected to get on the train to Manchester and take herself to one of the gaunt, sooty sanctity factories that ground the girls of the northwest into the pious paste of Catholic womanhood, that turned out Catholic mothers, Catholic nurses, Catholic teachers, all of them with an eye cocked for a good Catholic boy with whom they could collaborate to produce a new Catholic generation who could be ground in the same way. But this was of no interest to my mother. She wanted a bit of class.

The education authority said there was no debate about it; they wouldn't pay for Derbyshire girls to go to schools in Cheshire. They had made their arrangement with the Manchester schools, to accommodate the left-footers, the papists, the awkward squad; they weren't going to vary it. But my mother had set her heart on this school for me, and she and Jack—since they had to run somewhere—ran over the border and into the small town where the convent was situated. In that way, the problem was solved; but my mother, with pluck and verve, fought the battle with the education authority on behalf of those other little girls left behind. She did not believe in the Manchester convent schools; they were unfit establishments. The girls stole from one another, she said, their conduct and language were shocking; they had ground my cousin Beryl, and ground her into a good Catholic shorthand-typist. My mother envisaged something grander for me; and why shouldn't Hadfield girls have their chance? She'd had none; but she would make her name, battling this issue; she'd show she was a force to be reckoned with. Eventually a compromise was cobbled together, and on the first day of term, September 1963, a small glum band of Hadfield lasses stood on the edge of their posh new world. In retrospect, this was unfortunate for me. I had changed my surname to Jack's, and was pretending he was married to my mother, and that I was his daughter. I had to go on and on pretending it. The lasses knew better. They might be only eleven but they weren't complete idiots; otherwise, they'd have been Catholic failures, wouldn't they? Word spread.

For a while, the posh girls at the convent laughed at me: as much for my accent as because they heard rumors about my private life. There was an attempt, rather feeble, to bully me: thefts of my possessions, pages ripped out of my books by unseen hands. People say girls can be cruel, but it's nothing a smart slap on the jaw won't cure. Strangely, though, I didn't have to get violent at all. One day in the lunch hour, when the whole school, rain or shine, was turned out of doors for fresh air, I saw our Top Nun walking alone, on an eminence, a raised patch of ground; she was a tiny, fierce item, horribly feared— though I did not know it—by parents and pupils both; after Malachy, she seemed to me a pussy-cat. On New Parents' Day, we had been treated, mother and child, to a good thrash through the school rules and sumptuary laws; all uniform to be purchased from approved stockist, no hand-knitted or self-contrived items, no jewelry except holy medals, and no nail varnish or cosmetic adornment on pain of torture and death. After this telling-off, my mother had approached the Top Nun, strung up, somewhat subdued. She was worried that I was not physically robust, that I would be found wanting: she was afraid I was not plain enough, worried that my streak of ashy hair, which once again fell to my waist, would be flouting the rules against conventual simplicity. Seeing a mother heaving in view, a parent with the temerity to make an individual approach—a parent who had been told but not told hard enough—Sister gave a pained, ironic smile.

My mother indicated me. "She can't do games," she said. "Or P.E. The doctor . . ." Sister looked me over, where I shrank at my mother's elbow. "Gym?" she said mildly. "Well, we do find most girls are very unhappy if anything interrupts their gym." My mother nodded and nodded, sacrificing me within seconds on the altar of Most Girls: my colics and cramps, my pains and my panics. Then she burst out with her real, eager, zealot's question: "Long hair—is that all right. Shall I have her hair cut off?"

Sister Mary Francis stared at her for a moment, then gave a sweet giggle, like a little girl's. It was a sound I would wait many years to hear again: Oh heavens, she said. Oh, no, don't do that. That will be quite all right. Tied back, you know. Navy ribbon, if you must. Oh heavens . . . don't cut off her hair.

We were held in a moment—my mother and I—of blushing embarrassment. Perhaps only I blushed; my mother was a woman, and had face. And I imagined Sister, that night, going back to the company of her fellow nuns, putting her feet up, rolling her eyes, and exclaiming, "New parents! What are they like?"

So now, this misty November lunchtime, sorry for her solitary state, I approached her, and got chatting. Arrival at the convent had reduced me, once again, to a very little girl, a starter, with simple easy manners; hierarchies were never obvious to me, and I felt warmly toward this tiny Top Nun whose nose and lips were blue from cold. Had she not defended my hair? For two pins, my mother would have cropped my head, and sent me out looking like a convict; the girls would have said I had nits, if—at the Convent of the Nativity—they knew what nits were, and in any case the loss of my hair would have taken away my only distinction. I may—though I don't remember this clearly—have taken Top Nun's tiny poisoned hand in mine.

"Hilary," she said. (Top Nun aspirated.) "Yes," I said; we chatted a while. Was I managing the gym, she asked? Not really, I said, I was generally rather poor at hopping and frog jumps, but I was resigned to it. "However, while very happy generally, I have a complaint. Among other items, my shoe bag has vanished. My shoes in it."

"Have you had a good look for it?" Top Nun asked.

"Well," I said, "to the best of my powers. Shoes don't walk."

Top Nun seemed to inhale her thin lips. She looked up and surveyed her constituency. We stood together while her eyes raked her charges, some four hundred girls running on the spot and blowing on their hands and chafing their blue thighs to stimulate blood flow, girls laughing and running in girl gangs and mocking and chanting, girls flashing at one another illicit pictures of pop stars, girls gossiping and flocking and crowing and ill-behaving; girls, not a few of them, stopped and trans- fixed and looking our way. Top Nun paused, considering. "Do you know," she said, "I think that if you were to go and look again for your shoe bag, let's say, after school at four o'clock . . . I believe you would find, Hilary, that it is exactly where it ought to be."

What I felt, privately, was extreme anguish. I thought that my parents could not afford to replace my shoes, or anything else that was lost; what was worse than this thought, was the thought of breaking it to my mother that in this place the girls also stole, that shoes walked, that books ripped themselves, that you were powerless against the wider society or against what ghosts did when your back was turned: that we had come to a new town, a new house, and that we were still not safe and unmolested. I didn't want her to know that this place was like that place; she was hoping so desperately that all places were not the same, she had staked her name on it, she had picked us up and run with us to a place that now looked no safer than the one where we'd been before. Thank you Sister, I said politely. I'll have a look. Well, you know, she said. If all is not well, Hilary. Her glance flickered again over her charges, now moaning in a slashing icy drizzle, pulling their sweaters over their heads and scurrying into lines to be let into afternoon school. If all is not well, I shall be very surprised. She spoke with an accent like the queen's, but her upper lip was long, in the Irish style. She turned it up—blue as it was—into a tiny sadistic smirk.

It was well; of course it was. My shoe bag, by school-out time, was hanging on my allotted peg. My books were never torn again. It took me years to understand how the trick had been worked; that bold girls out to terrorize were so afraid of a sarcastic little sister that they were reduced to infantile compliance at the thought that she might be looking their way. I was learning, always learning: power is negotiated, acquired, given away, in more subtle ways than I had understood when gun law and the power of the sword were all that prevailed in my world. We must break down the barriers of deference, as Tom Paine tells us; this can be done quite politely, so that people don't see that you are dismantling the things and discreetly sneaking them away. My convent years left me a legacy: a nervous politeness, an appearance of feminine timidity which will probably stand me in good stead if I am ever on trial for murder.

As for Top Nun: I learned her ways, she mine. When I was in my last year at the convent, pupils and staff voted me in, democratic, no deals, no bribes: Top Girl. I was entitled to a gown of scarlet with a gold stripe, which I wore with an air of sarcasm. Every morning—this was the ritual of the Convent of the Nativity—I stood on the stage of our vast assembly hall—so big that it was hired out to Protestants for the Mayor's Ball and vast civic junkets—and at nine o'clock, as Top Nun took the stage, I would say, on behalf of us all, "Good morning, Sister Mary Francis."

Sometimes I was tremulous, because of things that were happening at home. Sometimes I was breathless, from belting in at the last minute, plunging my arms into the gown held by an underling, and vaulting onto the stage. Sometimes my tone was warm: if I'd had a good weekend. My hymn book sometimes had love letters tucked inside it: from Catholic boys, of course. I always, whatever, tried to greet her as if I meant it.

And she, speaking to me as if I were plural, and gazing out over the school, gazing into space, would reply, "Good morning girls." She spoke into empty air, neutral, faint: as if she were biting on some edgeless, metaphysical glass. She was beyond shame, beyond embarrassment. After Vatican II—the great church council during which the sainted John XXIII told nuns to get hip and raise their hemlines—the whole school saw her sparrow legs, encased in thick stockings but somehow naked to our gaze; we didn't even make jokes about it. The nuns, too, were told to get out and about, and so Top Nun tried to learn to drive. She should have crushed her instructors, her examiners, with force of will; we could not believe—word leaked out—that she had to take her test again and again. When finally she passed, I surprised her, after morning assembly, with a huge, rather vulgar bouquet. You girls should not have known, she hissed at me, before accepting the flowers with an injured, ungracious simper.

One day when I was seventeen, almost hatched, almost ready to fly, I was standing at dusk in one of our cloakrooms, brushing out my hair. We were off in fifteen minutes to an after-school function, to be bussed to Manchester to some other school—I can't remember which, and little it matters—for some interschool debating torment, tournament, something of that sort: I was our chief combatant, and because of this I had to show up in my uniform and all my friends—oh, sob, sniff— had gone home to change into their miniskirts and put on their eyeliner. I was feeling sorry for myself, and doing the one thing I could: so narcissistic that I was almost melting into the mirror, I was brushing out my hair. I planned to wear it loose; who would say I couldn't? I sighed at myself: who is like me? Nobody has hair like this. Oh, what they would give! Brush and brush. I prolonged the strokes so that each segment was drawn out by the brush to its fullest length, before I released it, and let it fall to join the fading light. Then I saw behind me, in the mirror, a black-and-white dwarf. It was SMF, Sister Mary Francis, Top Nun, crouching like a court freak in the top of the frame: as if Velázquez had painted us. Her eyes locked into mine. "Ready?" she said, unpleasantly. "I was just . . ." my voice faded. Her coldest curl of the lip said, she knew what I was just. Just admiring myself, just doing a fair old Magdalen impersonation. I felt caught out, diminished; yet made real, fleshy, sordid.

But Sister had a lot invested in the debating competition. For the first time, our little school was on the way to winning. You didn't pick your subject, or your side. On the night when Sister caught me, I was preparing to debate the proposition we had drawn out of a hat: "Karl Marx has done more for humanity than Jesus Christ." I walked it. The final, everyone felt, was a formality; the strongest opposing team had been trampled into the dust.

Back at school, where our bus set us down, my friends pulled me to the convent door. Emboldened by three vodka-and-limes, a comrade studded her finger on the bell. The door fell open, nuns fell out, some of them with young and eager faces. "Did ye win?"

Oh yes, my friends said. Communists one, Christians nil. Sister Mary Francis whisked around a corner, like a nasty sprite, and put her hand on my sleeve, and looked up into my face; once again I heard that giggle, sweet and clear as a running stream.

Here are some things that Jack did not agree with: breakfast, sport, and illness.

He himself went out of the house in the morning on just half a cup of tea, which, my mother said, he could barely stomach.

Weaker people—that is, me—were allowed tea and toast.

Sport was rubbish, except for professional wrestling, which he watched on TV. History was bunk. Illness was bunk. In the entire course of his school career, he had been "never absent, never late."

But now Mr. Neverill had become stepfather to Miss Neverwell, which was unfortunate for both of them. Jack had forgotten his colic, the colic he'd had something chronic. I had almost loved him, so long ago when he had told my mother to let me stay home. It was a near thing, quite near to love; that momentary tenderness, when I was nine, my baby body pausing at the foot of the slope of womanhood. But now he said, when I came downstairs one Monday morning, my uniform tie skewed, my flesh gray, and my teeth chattering, feel *ill,* do you? Easy for *you* to say! I *also* feel ill on a Monday morning! But I have to bloody *work,* don't I? Have to do it!

I sat down at the table. Surely my mother would see what ailed me? It was the war between men and women; she had to pick sides, and I could tell by her face that she wouldn't be picking mine. It was already a weakness in my case that I was hanging about, that I was sitting down and no doubt wanting

some toast; for Jack was perfect and so was his morning nausea, a spiritual quality I should try to emulate. Accordingly, she
drew back in her chair and frowned at me, her eyes running up
and down my body, and found fault with my appearance altogether, my lank hair which was without its ribbon and the
run in my stocking that I had twisted to the inside to disguise it.
Could it possibly be true, she said, that the school said I should
wear stockings? Mm, I said, s'true; perhaps my hand fumbled
for the copy of the rules I kept always in the bottom corner of my
satchel, the folded paper creased and worn and dyed a pinkish-
tan where the color of the leather had bled into it. She didn't
think it *could* be true, she said while I rummaged around among
my books. She couldn't see Sister taking that line at all. Should
I not, at my age, still be wearing the uniform woolen kneesocks,
for which she had paid so dear at the approved supplier when I
was in Form I?

It was a humiliating question. The answer was no; I was, by
the rules, now graduated out of kneesocks. Once you've graduated you can't go back to them, any more than you can reverse
your age and undo puberty. The difficulty in my life was that
stockings were a continuing, unforeseen expense. I had no
income of my own. I had savings in a money box, from what
my grandparents gave me. But the box was not there for my
own use; it was for my mother to crack open, when Jack was in
too bad a temper to be asked for ready cash. Stockings or tights
should be at least 30 denier, the school rules said, and of the
approved shade. My mother was unwilling to invest in such
durable garments. Bet your life Cinderella never wore 30 denier.
She gifted me her cast-off nylons, the threads already running
at the toe; and here we were, Monday morning, locked in common hatred, the tea cooling, the little boys banging above as
they flopped out of bed, and Jack pushing back his chair from

the table, muttering, his eyes downturned, perhaps wondering, as I did, how did we get into this? I shuffled back my own chair to give me space, like someone about to stand up and start a fight. I considered the expression "for two pins." For two pins I'd land a punch.

Two pins were often necessary to secure my drooping sanitary arrangements; certainly they would be today. Jack was still muttering as he flung himself out into the morning, to take out his feelings on the poor car standing shivering in the drive; to twist its key as if he were twisting its ear, to stamp his foot on the gas and make the engine snarl, to grind the gears. Our cars were always starting mutinies in those years, coughing to a stubborn halt at the roadside, blowing their tires and careering downhill. A machine, as far as Jack was concerned, was like a fellow human, and could be terrorized in the same way. Show it your fist, the bloody bastard: that will bring it into line.

Jack seldom swore, except at what was inanimate. He cursed the fire when it wouldn't light, come on, you bloody bastard, come on. If any household object stuck, jammed, snapped, or came to pieces, it could expect no quarter from Jack. I said to my Polish friend Anne, whose calm intelligence I valued, "You see, I am never like that. I don't get unreasonably angry—only reasonably so. I would never, ever be beating up the furniture, or cursing the step if I'd stubbed my toe, or shouting at the tires because the road has worn them bald."

"Well, Hilary," Anne said, her sardonic glance sliding sideways: "I think that's very fair-minded of you."

My mother and I had a vacuum cleaner, mail order from a pay-as-you-go catalogue. Hoover Constellation was its name; when it was young, its cylinder—a novelty then—bobbed behind you like a puppy. We listened to its every note as you would to a baby's cry, we stopped it before its engine overheated, we soothed it and pampered it and fitted it with new bags, and when its hose split we mended it with sticky tape, till there was more tape than the original hose. By these means, we made it run for many years. But the Constellation was our one big success; our domestic arrangements were always on the verge of collapsing. When we moved into our house at Romiley, Jack made the purchase of an automatic washing machine. It was the latest technology, and so it soon broke down. We were not allowed to call in a repairman, for they are all cheats. So we did the washing in the bath, my mother and me. In those days when the world was polluted men and boys wore their shirts for three days till the collars were black inside and filmed with a sort of industrial grease. The only way to get rid of it was to rub so hard you abraded the fibers, wearing out the garment in the process. I never minded this; I was a short-term thinker. But rub with what, was the question? My mother would not purchase a block of laundry soap, only the powder with which she had fed, so briefly, the Wondermatic machine. Our hot water was not hot enough to dissolve the powder; it clumped on the gray-white pockets of my brothers' shirts, around the collars and hems, so that I had to flick it away with my fingers, shake it off as I lifted their dripping garments; which now, lengthened and weighted, looked almost priestlike. The Wondermatic stayed on show, to impress any stray visitor. In time my mother flung a tablecloth over it, so that it was raised from perfect uselessness to the dignity of table. Then Jack built a sort of house for it, a hinged flap which covered its top and gave us extra working space. How did we wash our blankets? I don't know that people ever did. My smallest brother developed allergies, blue-faced coughs and wheezes; my mother responded by heaping more blankets on him, and placing a plug-in radiator by his bed, so the dust mites could breed better. She and Jack moved their double bed into his room for a time, so they could give him medicine in the night and share the benefit of the extra warmth. I lived in the healthy cold of the box room. Once, experimentally, I set up a thermometer, bringing it downstairs when I was twelve and still naïve, to say look Mum, almost freezing point!

When my future husband came into our lives, he observed the problem, bundled up me and the washing, tipped us into his student's car and took us to the Laundromat. My mother marveled at the results, though she seldom funded our trips; she seemed to think it all happened naturally. Waiting for the cycles to finish, I learned how the wet heat exacerbated the pains in my legs. Go to the pub and get a Guinness, I'd urge my boyfriend, while I wait for this lot to dry. I was happy to send him away for the sheer pleasure of seeing him again. One night, slumped on the slatted wooden seat, I looked up from my novel as he came back through the swinging glass door. I said, this book I'm reading says that Johannesburg has the most perfect climate in the world. The woman, the character, she is sitting on her balcony, it is midwinter, the sun is shining, she worries about politics, her conscience tells her she should go into exile, but. The world's most hateful regime, I said, has the most beautiful climate.

I shook my head, wondering at the perversity of nature. He scooped out the clothes from the dryers into my ready arms, and my body warmed as I held them, through my ribs from front to back; my legs still ached with an old singing pain, which could not be, surely—could not by now be growing pains? I imagined the sun, the balcony, the scarlet flowers spilling from their pots; the torrid world of the curtains, when the curtains were drawn. Could we go there, I said? I don't mind anywhere really, somewhere hot or somewhere cold, jungle or tundra is all the same to me. Somewhere else.

A big question of Jack's was this: why are women always smiling? Look at them, he would say, pointing to the television screen. Smile, smile, smile.

Jack banned Shakespeare and mashed potato. Shakespeare was a subject, not a person. It was an unfortunate prescription of weak-minded women schoolteachers. It was an exam subject and could be tolerated if kept between the covers of my *Complete Works*, but it was not permitted to leak out into the real world—it should not be viewed on television, and especially not when it clashed with the wrestling. Shakespeare, when it occurred, was on the BBC. Wrestling was not. The BBC was bunk.

Potatoes should be chips or plain boiled in big chunks. It was forbidden to squash your potato surreptitiously with the side of your fork.

I was in trouble for sitting too close to the fire, "pretending to be cold." I was in trouble for being a girl, for being thirteen, for being fourteen. All my behavior seemed to anger him, just by the fact of *being* behavior: but silences, absences, were also a provocation to him. I have heard of fathers who said their daughters would grow up to be whores, or hairdressers. Jack said that I would grow up to be a lab assistant. This would be my fate if my math didn't improve. It didn't seem to occur to Jack that I might have a career outside the sciences; perhaps he didn't think there was one. There were only little jobs that women did: smile, smile, smile.

Life was a hair shirt to Jack. Like me, my mother claimed, he had been forced against his natural grain. His youth had been an unhappy one; his father had deserted his family and Jack had been forced too early out of education and into a job, into earning money for his mother and his younger sister. Given his choice, she said, he would never have been an engineer; he would rather have been an artist. Forgive me, I would say under my breath, if I'm a little skeptical here. What would Jack say if he saw any signs of artistry in me?

Yet we had never forgotten his big success. I had been nine, maybe ten, when Jack's article on physical culture was published in *Health & Strength,* when the letter of congratulation came in, "Yours, Oscar." His article began in this way: "PC is the Aunt Sally of the sporting world." I thought that a dashing turn of phrase. I experimented with its meaning. Probably only someone London-born, like Jack, would know anything about an Aunt Sally. Was it a target everyone threw at? At some Cockney sporting fair? Was a target not a legitimate aim? Was Sally some doll you knocked over? I turned it about and about. Ilary is the Aunt Sally of the sporting world. Sally is of the sporting world the Ilary. Jack got a book from the library, called *Teach Yourself Freelance Writing.* It had a black-and-yellow jacket; I turned it over in my hands, I looked into it. I read all his library books, though they were usually science fiction. Use good grammar, it said; be original. My mother's books were historical novels, their contents sometimes quite louche. I thought I could write a book, from the commandments I'd acquired: use good grammar: be original: be historical. I wrote a few lines of my projected book. Disconcertingly to me, it was in dialogue, but I didn't know who was talking, or quite where; it seemed to be Belgium, but I didn't think they had Belgium. Flanders then? It was definitely a seaport; I could hear the gulls, and see a man in dark garments lurking on the steps of a church. I said to my mother, Henry VII is interesting. No he's not, my mother said.

I said, I like the imposters you see, the pretenders to the crown, I could write a book about that, except you can't have a book about someone called Perkin Warbeck; that's a bit of a blight on the whole thing, you know, a hero called Perkin? But I thought I would like to have a book on the library shelves with my name on its spine, its plastic cover bubbling, the corners of its pages broken, yellow, thumbed. When I was fourteen, I was loosed at last into the adult library, given six tickets of my own to choose what I liked. A library lady followed me, trailing me around the shelves, smiling and offering to help. "You may find it bewildering," she said, "so much choice!" I gave her a furious stare, edged away pointedly. *For two pins* I would have knocked her flat to the dusty parquet.

Unlike the doctor, Jack didn't name me. Once I had been Ilary, but after I was fifteen or so he called me they. "They always do this," or "they always that," he would sneer. I felt as if I were a survival, a relic, a small squat subject race, whose aboriginal culture was derided; like the Welsh, for example, a nation for whom Jack had no time at all. Suppose you had grown up speaking Welsh, but now its use was prohibited. Even if you were obedient, if you were too scared to break the law, you would go on having Welsh thoughts, and the powers-that-be would always be scrutinizing you, for evidence of subversion on your face. When you were silent, they'd be looking for clicks of your tongue and contractions of your jaw, to see if you were dissenting. They'd be listening at doors, to find out if you talked in your sleep.

Jack liked the people around him to be in the same frame of mind as he was. So if he was tense, injured, and gloomy, you would be in trouble if you went calmly about your business. If he was in the mood to be jocular, the whole household must sit before the TV set and roar at some low comedian. I kept out of the TV circle, and stayed in the dining room with my homework. He said, "They never laugh."

I would shut myself away and write history essays, derivative in content but of formidable length and grubby appearance. The pen called Swann moved as if it were writing on water; you wrote, and hardly felt the grain of the paper. But the use of Swann was many years behind me, and we were not big on office supplies when I grew up. When I was sixteen I wrote in leaking and blotchy Biro, a hundred pages of black bad handwriting, the quarto sheets held together—for want of staples or paperclips—with embroidery silk that I picked up from my mother's offcuts: coral, fern-green, the scarlet shade of the tip of butterflies' wings. The silk looked grimy after I'd twisted it up with my inky fingers, after I'd carried the pages about for a few days, scuffling footnotes into place and scratching second thoughts in the margin. Truth isn't pretty, I thought, and the pursuit of it doesn't make pretty people. Truth isn't elegant; that's just mathematicians' sentimentality. Truth is squalid and full of blots, and you can only find it in the accumulation of dusty and broken facts, in the cellars and sewers of the human mind. History's what people are trying to hide from you, not what they're trying to show you. You search for it in the same way you sift through a landfill: for evidence of what people want to bury.

There was tension in the air of our house, like the unbreathing stillness between the lightning and the thunder. In this space I went to and fro, clutching my essays with their slipping knots and scattering pages. Thin and pale, with long legs and a long fall of colorless hair, I was impeccably suited to my era, though the sixties were late in coming to the north. The girls at school were always combing through their biology textbooks to find something wrong with me. I was hyperthyroid perhaps, or anemic. Envy was the name of their disease.

Those were years of financial struggle for my family, and strange expedients to make money. Appearances had to be kept up, and our history suppressed. People now will ask, what's so wrong, what's so difficult about running away and changing your names? But there were big problems in that era, especially if you only ran away for about eight miles: even if it was eight miles over the county boundary into Cheshire. In provincial England at that time, if you didn't want trouble you had to be like everyone else. If for some reason you weren't the genuine article, you became a pretender, an imposter; imposting not for a day or a week, but simulating as a profession, simulating as a way of life. If you were living with someone you weren't married to—even if, and especially if, you were still married to someone else—you called yourself just a regular family and hoped people bought into your fictions; but at any time a person who knew better might come along and explode them. My brothers remembered little or nothing of their early history. Jack brought them up and Jack was their father. They were English, without religion, and without a Hadfield accent. Because I was enrolled at a convent school I was nominally a Catholic, outwardly conforming, though all—even Top Nun—knew my views. After my bad time in the secret garden, my *mauvais quart d'heure,* I stopped believing in an omnipotent God; I believed in him as a pretty conceit for a year into high school, but I didn't credit him with much pull, and after I was twelve I didn't believe in him at all. And as my great-uncles and great-aunts died one by one, I lost my consciousness of being

Irish. The Hadfield accent never completely shifted, but it was my long memory that was the problem. The past could not be knocked or pulled out of me. It seemed to be knitted into my nervous system; I recalled conversations from long ago, even conversations I had never heard. I was troubled by dreams of alien but familar cities, by mental pictures that were insistent but unresolved. A man in dark garments lurks on the steps of a church.

As the decade wore on and my family became established in its new life, I felt like a death's-head at a feast. Henry, my father, might as well have been dead; except that the dead were more discussed. Perhaps my mannerisms recalled him, as an unwelcome ghost by the fire: the clerkly droop of the head, the habit of reading a book as if your eyes were hoovering the words from the page.

He was never mentioned after we parted: except by me, to me. We never met again.

After my first week at the convent, I went home to my mother, worried. "Big girls at school," I told her, "ask me why I've changed my name." (Eight miles: a county boundary: Catholic gossip permeates civic barriers, runs freely between parish and parish, an underground polluted stream.)

"Tell them," she said, "that it's for private reasons."

I tried out this turn of phrase: private reasons. "Oh yes," the big girls said. "We understand that. But we want to know what they are."

Once you have learned habits of secrecy, they aren't so easy to give up. That is why this chapter is shorter than it might be. When I was growing up, my stepfather, Jack, lived in an emotional labyrinth through which I could not begin to follow him.

I knew a bit of his story then, I know a little more now; it may be, though, that what I think I know is misleading, and now is not the time for it, and here is not the place. Jack was a person who was loyal to what he believed; in those years, his mind was never changed. Facts in which he had faith were invested with great emotional weight—facts indeed were judgments, and if you knew a contrary fact you had better keep very quiet about it, since mere possession of it was an offense. Even when he was wrong he was right; that was the arrangement. His status as father and wage earner gave him a moral rightness that was separate from accuracy or even likelihood. He was right because he was entitled to be right.

I learned from Marx how the brute facts of economic interaction underlie our notion of human nature. I wished Marx would come for his tea and bring Engels, and that they would sit and squash their potatoes and see how far they got.

When I was eighteen I left home to go to the London School of Economics. My course was law, and my burning desire for equity made me peculiarly unsuited to the subject.

Show Your Workings

B y the time I was twenty I was living in a slum house in Sheffield. I had a husband and no money; those things I could explain. I had a pain which I could not explain; it seemed to wander about my body, nibbling here, stabbing there, flitting every time I tried to put my finger on it.

When I packed my bags for London, at eighteen years old, I went to live in a women's hall of residence in Bloomsbury. It was a haven of warmth, calm, and order. My university course was engrossing, and it was taught by lawyers and academics of stature and reputation. I got involved in student politics, in meetings that dragged on toward midnight. I didn't think it was a waste of time; student politics at the LSE had at least some crossover with the real world. The school was mostly post-graduate, and cosmopolitan. Whatever foreign event made the news, there was someone who would tell you about it, explain the background from their own experience. The rattling, down-at-heel, overcrowded buildings pleased me better than any grassy quad or lancet window. And I was doing well; my tutors were beginning to talk to me about where my interests lay, about how I might like to specialize, in my third year. One of them invited me into his office, which was the size of a modest broom cupboard, and said, go in for constitutional law, constitutional and administrative, you'll study under Professor Griffith; that's my strong recommendation to you. How do we delimit authority, where do the powers of the state begin and end? My path seemed to have taken a new turn; it seemed I was a step or two from success. I hugged myself and thanked my tutor, but I walked away thinking, third year, third year, by then I won't be here.

There are times in life when the next, clear, logical step seems one you can't take at all. I found it difficult to see myself completing my course, and emerging as a grown-up London person on the verge of a career. I seemed to have less money than other people. I had the state grant and—in theory at least—the small yearly contribution that my parents should make. I schemed to do without that contribution, to spare them the expense, but my schemes didn't work. The hall fees took a huge slice out of my grant and left me with little room for incidentals, but they covered heat and light, breakfast and supper; in between came a pot of yogurt. In my second year, I was aware, I would not be able to stay in hall and would have to find somewhere of my own to live. Any place I could afford would be well outside the city center, so I would have to budget for fares, instead of walking everywhere as I did at present. In those days, students didn't generally get term-time jobs to supplement their grants; your course demanded your full-time commitment. Intermittently through my first year, I worried about this, and about something more serious and long-term. I wanted to be a barrister. How was I to do this? The facts of life pressed in on me. I was female, northern, and poor. My family would not be able to help me through my postdegree studies, or my pupilage—that is to say, the barrister's apprenticeship. Women barristers were then in a small minority. A few brave women from unhelpful backgrounds had crashed the system. I had assumed I would be one of them. But now my resolve was undermined. I was acquainted with the facts of life, with some unpromising arithmetic. Also, I was in love.

I had known this a while before I came to London, but by the time the calamitous fact was admitted, between myself and the boy who was in it with me, we had already chosen our universities, and secured places at different ends of England. He had just turned eighteen, I was six months younger. We couldn't do anything about the parting that loomed ahead of us, but we had decided to be married, whenever it looked possible: sooner than that, if by any mischance I became pregnant. When we had a daughter, my lover said, he would like to call her Catriona; would that be all right by me? I was very happy about it. We were both admirers of Robert Louis Stevenson. *Kidnapped* was really our favorite, but we couldn't call our daughter David, or name her after Alan Breck. She'd have to be named for the sequel.

Like all my contemporaries, in those first years when the contraceptive pill was widely available, I only half-believed I could coerce my body, and suspected that it might have some filthy tricks in store; but the filthy tricks would be on the line of putting a baby in your arms before you were ready. I assumed I would be able to have Catriona at a time of my choosing. I didn't know she would always be a ghost of possibility, a paper baby, a person who slipped between the lines. It's a pity we didn't like *Travels with a Donkey*. There's a good name for a ghost: Modestine.

In our year apart my boyfriend and I wrote to each other every day. There was a hiatus when the postmen went on national strike; I don't think it was to protest at us personally, though some of the letters were very weighty. In later years, we carried the correspondence about with us, in a plastic bin bag, but when we first went to work abroad we threw it away. After all, we were planning never to be parted again.

Though I was happy in my London life, I looked forward with a sick intensity to his arrival for weekend visits. He had to be smuggled in, and kept like contraband in my room, my roommate quartered elsewhere and a whole corridor of girls sworn to complicit secrecy; it was like Malory Towers, but with sex. When the girl along the corridor had a boyfriend stay with her, the fire alarm rang in the small hours, and I met her among the crowds on Malet Street, two hundred girls turned out in their night attire into the winter cold. Her face was white, her eyes were staring; "Where is he?" I whispered, and she hissed, "I put him in the wardrobe."

The expense of traveling, the logistical maneuvers required, the wear and tear on the nerves, meant that the visits had to be well spaced out. And gradually, I realized that my world was changing. Light and color were draining from the streets, and even spring didn't restore it. The gray ache of absence was too much to bear; why bear it, if it could be remedied? I thought it could. By early summer, when my surroundings had taken on the chewed, grainy monochrome of crumpled newsprint, I went to the university authorities to put my case. Did they think I could go up to Sheffield, and continue my course there? My boyfriend couldn't come to me, I explained, because he was studying geology, and geology isn't portable. He had already chosen his mapping area and walked it at weekends, and it was easier to move one law student with a suitcase than to relocate a massive chunk of carboniferous limestone from the Peak District, four square miles of rock swarming with corals, nautiloids, and the ancestors of starfish.

Sheffield University's law faculty was housed, in 1971, in a former maternity home, with ramshackle partitions and makeshift corridors. The students seemed dull, hostile, and pitifully young; they were my own age, in fact, but I felt I had different experiences and was older. They were afraid of their teachers, and before tutorials they stood in rigid knots outside closed doors, waiting, tension building between them; those rooms, full of the awe and anticipation of women's pain, were now darkened by juvenile dread of donnish sarcasm. But "donnish" is pitching it too high perhaps; one of my tutors was a bored local solicitor who made it plain that he didn't think women had any place in his classroom. They were just a waste of space; they'd only go and have babies, wouldn't they?

Some people have forgotten, or never known, why we needed the feminist movement so badly. This was why: so that some talentless prat in a nylon shirt couldn't patronize you, while around you the spotty boys smirked and giggled, trying to worm into his favor. The birth control revolution of the late sixties had passed our elders by—educators and employers both. It was assumed that marriage was the beginning of a woman's affective life, and the end of her mental life. It was assumed that she neither could nor would exercise choice over whether to breed; poor silly creature, no sooner would her degree certificate be in her hand before she'd cast all that book learning to the winds, and start swelling and simpering and knitting bootees. When you went for a job interview, you would be asked, if you were not wearing a wedding ring, whether you were engaged; if you were engaged or married, you would be asked when you intended to "start your family." Whether you were celibate, or gay, or just a sensible preplanner, you had to smile and jump through the flaming hoops held up for you by some grizzled ringmaster, shifty and semi-embarrassed as he asked a girl half his age to tell him about her sex life and account for her next ovulation.

My transfer to Sheffield University was not as smooth as I had hoped. On paper, my first and second year fitted together. In practice, they didn't. While the LSE was occupied in wrenching its first-year law studies into some sort of social context, Sheffield was sneaking in extra property law, under the guise of legal history. I found myself at sea, both baffled and bored. My fellow second-years mostly intended to be solicitors. They were going into daddy's practice, or into their uncle's. I got into trouble by claiming mischievously that jurisprudence was all an elaborate bluff and that legal language was cognate with magic. "Sign your name here or make your mark: pronounce a formula: abracadabra, you are man and wife. I put on a wig, I indict a scroll: abracadabra, your marriage is dissolved." If you are right, said my tutor heavily, I suppose we may as well all go home. He stood up and clasped his arms behind his back, and looked out of his window, melancholy, toward the distant hills.

All the same, Sheffield was a good place to be if you were a student. The townspeople talked to you at the bus stop and in the shops, and they didn't seem to have any money either, so you could buy cheap cuts of meat and bargain tins and sustaining fresh loaves hot from the oven. Do you realize, I would ask my boyfriend, that at your tender age of nineteen, you both run a car and keep a mistress? The car was the product of his summer working in a factory that made cardboard boxes; his hands sliced to pieces, but pound notes stacking up. The car's laboring engine often jibbed at Sheffield's steep hills, and gaping holes in its bodywork were patched with a substance called plastic padding, but it hauled us across the moors to see his family; we made the trip often, as his father was sick. I cooked for us every night at my lodging, an attic room in the house of a kindly, absentminded divorced woman who didn't mind that two of us were trooping up her stairs.

There were two electric rings in my room, one for our carbohydrate of the day—pasta, rice, potatoes—one for our meat or fish. We were ingenious cooks, and sat smiling over our yellow Formica table, as our dinner bubbled and simmered; I would be shivering slightly, because the only means of ventilation was an open window that admitted the piercing wind. One day, as I was hauling a great bag of potatoes uphill, my landlady stopped me at the gate. Her brow was furrowed. "Ilary," she said, "why are you doing this?" I dumped my bag at my feet, and smiled up at her, bent double, massaging my carrying arm. "You should be going out," she said.

I flew out of myself, saw myself through her eyes: a small pale child with cropped hair, wearing a coat outgrown by one of her younger brothers. "It's all right," I said. "Don't worry, I'm fine."

I never quite understood what this was, this "going out." What was the gratification in it? It seemed to me, generally, just a polite prelude to sex; if you've got beyond politeness, why get dressed up and go off into the cold? You have a person you want to be with, who you'd rather be with than be on your own; isn't that, by itself, a sort of fiesta? As for the grocery shopping: I liked to be able to say we ate well, that we stretched our small amount of money as far as a proper meal every night. There was nothing left over. And besides, I was trying to feed us up, trying to pad us against the disaster to come. That was a dark winter; the miners were on strike, and there were long cold hours without electricity. On a January night, we were called home, and the expected death occurred.

My boyfriend's father was called Henry. He was fifty-three, a professional man, wry and studious, a father of five. In summer he was a well man and in September he was sick and the following January he was dead: cancer. A year later, to the day, my grandfather would die of the same disease; more winter journeys, over the dark Pennines, to stand about in hospital wards while screens were drawn around beds. But we were married by then, and living in a rented room over a garage, a jerry-built extension with a leaking roof; and when we returned from the funeral, we found that the cracks in the wall had grown wide, and that an aggressive black mold had grown on our food and on our clothes.

Married, why? Because in times of disaster, it's what you do. When families are destroyed suddenly, you pick yourselves up and glue yourselves together to form new units. More practically, and immediately, we married so that we could spend the night together, so that he did not have to roll out of bed and roll home over the midnight cobblestones; even the kindly divorcée, thinking of her two growing children and their moral development, would not let me have a man in the house till dawn. We had tried to find a place together, in anticipation of our marriage, but the landlords demanded certificates from the university, endorsements, and validation on oath to say that we had really truly booked the priest and the registrar. They wanted no fornication among their Formica, they were not about to yield one curling inch of their old linoleum to the mad young seeking to gratify themselves. In mouse-dropping hallways we pleaded our purity of intent. But the faces were stony with rectitude: no room at the inn.

Yet not everyone was hostile to romance. Some comfortable soul could always be found, in those days, to recall, "They say two can live as cheaply as one." Can they? My family fell out with me, and didn't fill in the forms for my subsistence grant. So we were about to find out if the saying was true.

Seventy-eight Roebuck Road was a back-to-back house; that is to say, it was one room deep, with a cellar, a room, a room on top of that, and an attic. It had one cold-water sink, a shared outside lavatory, and a single metered gasfire. Even the hardy cockroach gave it the go-by, but a darting population of creatures we used to call "silverfish" lived in the old chimney breast; they were harmless, I said to my husband, we used to have them at Brosscroft, they're okay, not dirty. I counted Roebuck Road as one of the greatest pieces of luck ever to come my way. We had not been able to afford the room over the garage: still less, the extra we might have been charged for growing the black mold. One of my tutors—a woman—had told me about a cheaper prospect; her cleaning lady lived there, but was moving on to something grander.

No. 78 was the cheapest house in the world. We had to go right across town every fortnight to pay the rent, but the car took us, and even we, having paid the rent, could afford to eat. My grandmother gave us a water-boiler to hang over the sink. My new mother-in-law gave us a cooker and some furniture. We slept on a sofa that flattened in the middle and so made into a bed. We couldn't get the stately family wardrobe upstairs, so it stayed down, its fine mirror reflecting the flickering of the silverfish as they busied cheerfully about their lives. I made stews, pies, cherry cakes, chocolate cakes, and chocolate cherry cakes. I answered, as law students do, my weekly "problems," in the set legal language, and each week turned out essays which were simply a more prolonged exercise in sifting and shuffling the same chary formulations. I complained that law was wrecking my English style, which had been sturdy by the time I was sixteen, a little oak tree: that it was teaching me to equivocate and hedge, to stick to the literal and to lower my intellectual sights.

I complained I had a pain in my legs, and I went to the doctor: and that was my big mistake.

Writing about your past is like blundering through your house with the lights fused, a hand flailing for points of reference. You locate the stolid wardrobe, and its door swings open at your touch, opening on the cavern of darkness within. Your hand touches glass, you think it is a mirror, but it is the window. There are obstacles to bump and trip you, but what is more disconcerting is a sudden empty space, where you can't find a handhold and you know that you are stranded in the dark. Each day I was taking, though I didn't know it, a small step toward the unlit terrain of sickness, a featureless landscape of humiliation and loss. At Roebuck Road, the stairhead was dark; and some previous occupant had pinned, on the blank wall you saw as you descended, a poster with an owl on it. It was a child's owl, a simple and almost a cartoon owl, not less baleful for that. I wanted to rip it down, but I couldn't reach it.

Letters from the Inland Revenue arrived, tax demands addressed to a "Mr. Judas Priest." These made us laugh. I set out my aspirin, one two three four five six. I swallowed them. Once, in error, I picked up and almost swallowed a shirt button, lying on the table waiting for me to sew it on.

"Sick?" said the doctor, down at the Student Health Service. "Throw up? I'm hardly surprised. You do know that taking six aspirin is no more effective than taking three?"

I didn't. As it was double any ordinary pain, I'd thought I could double the aspirin. We weren't very sophisticated in those days. I don't think we even had paracetamol. I had a big bottle of a hundred aspirin, and I used to take whatever number I thought would get me through the day.

"Well, Miss——" said the doctor. He glanced down at his file, and a little jolt shot through him, as if he were electrified. "Mrs.?" he said. "Mrs.? You've got married? Pregnant, are you?"

I hope not, I thought. If so, I've overdone it with the aspirin. It'll have fins. Or feathers. Three extra aspirins, three extra heads. I'll exhibit it. It will keep us in luxury.

"I'm on the Pill," I said. An urge rose in me, to say, we are sexually very keen so I take three pills a day; do you think that's enough? But then a stronger urge rose in me, to be sick on his shoes.

I can see him, now that the years have flown; his crinkly fairish hair sheared short, his rimless glasses, his highly polished brogues. He was a nervous man, and when I bowed my head toward his feet he shifted them under his desk. I wasn't sick, not there and then. I put my hand across my mouth, and went outside, and threw up in the Student Health Service lavatories. It was quite a luxurious vomit, private and well lit. At Roebuck Road, our facility was shared with next door, and you had to plow down their garden to get to it, so that at night dogs barked and householders with their torches came out shouting,

"What's all this?" and you were caught in the cross beams, your loo-roll in your hand.

I went home. "What did the doctor say?" my husband asked.

"He said, don't take so many aspirin. I said my legs ached and he said it was accounted for by no known disease. Except one called idiopathic something-something."

I didn't say how I had grinned, when he said "idiopathic." I knew it meant, disease about which we doctors have no bloody idea. So he had bridled, and swallowed the rest of the medical term; he wasn't, anyway, entertaining it as a possibility, he was just boasting, showing he remembered his textbooks. And my smile called his bluff; I shouldn't have smiled it. He was not on my side now. I thought that probably he never had been.

Go back, said my mister, grimly. You haven't really told him. How tired you are. And how upset.

I was upset, it was true. I couldn't bear my smashed relationship with my family. That my brothers should think badly of me. That I should have no money to buy a present for Father's Day, only a bag of toffee, and nothing to give for Christmas but a box of biscuits and a bottle of wine.

That I had money to give even these was because of the intervention of a bureaucrat at County Hall in Chester, where lived the authority who paid (or not) my maintenance grant. For my visit I composed myself into pliant, pleading mode. We went to Chester by way of the grumbling, grunting, plastic-padded car. I went to see him in his office, the necessary man, the bureaucrat who was on my case. I explained that my father hadn't signed my forms to testify to his income. So therefore, he said, I could get no grant, not even the fifty pounds that every student got, even the rich ones: for those were the rules. I know this, I said, but you see I shall just have to sit here till the rules

Giving Up the Ghost

are amended in my favor, because if I don't get some money from you I'm out of house and home.

I don't remember his face, only his office, his desk, his chair, the slant of the light. He left the room. I studied his carpet, on which I had sworn I would be sleeping: unless I slept on his desk. It was a warm, blossoming, summer day: perhaps I could sleep in a flower bed? Sunlight rippled on magnolia walls. He came back smiling. I have got you fifty, he said, and let's see, hereafter, maybe it can be worked—there are always some strange circumstances . . .

Perhaps he was an angel. Perhaps a mortal, but one of the elect. I'm praying for him still, in a wild agnostic fashion. Hoping he wins the national lottery: I pray some irregular prayer like that. Or that he'd come to see me and I could make him a pie or a cake.

Go back, said my husband; tell them how you really are. Here you go, said the doctor, scribbling me a prescription; I think what you need is some antidepressants. I was depressed, so I knew it made a kind of sense. Twenty-four hours later, I found I couldn't read; print blurred before my eyes. I went to the university library and tried to look up the side effects of the drug, but I was laboring under the obvious handicap. In those days, pills didn't come with a patient information leaflet. Your doctor had all the information you needed, and whether you could get it depended on whether you had pull, face, and cunning. I had none of these.

I went to see my tutor in Equity, and said, look, Mr. Loath (it wasn't his name, I didn't say it, it was just what the frightened spotty boys called him), look, Loath, I'm coming to your next session, but don't harass me, right? (Really, of course, I spoke to him much more nicely than this.) Loath, please understand that I've been prescribed some necessary drugs that mean I can't read my books. Blurred vision. Side effects, I said. Under my breath: you must have heard of side effects? Loath gave me a puzzled look, as if he'd never heard of any such thing.

I tried some other tutors. I was asking for a week's grace, or perhaps a fortnight's, to audit my courses but not take part. Their reaction was all the same: why was I telling them this? The medical textbook (if I'd read it right, squinting, aslant) suggested that the blurred vision would last only a week or two, whereas the course of drugs lasted six weeks. Six weeks, in clinical practice, was the term set to depression; six weeks was a cure. After that, I was sure, I'd be happy. Never mind who was dead and how. Never mind how few the coins in my purse. I'd be up with the lark, and rejoicing with the wrens: I'd be skipping up the hills of Sheffield, my pains vanished, my joints springing, swinging my bags of potatoes and self-raising flour as if they were feathers, as if I were self-raised myself: and scattering my careless laughter to the winds. For the time being, though, my spirits had sunk. The drugs seemed to be having an effect, but not the one required. The pangs of bereavement, of estrangement, had given way to a dull apathy. My sleep was broken and the climate of my dreams was autumnal, like the dim leaf-mold interior of a copse; their content was exhausting and yet somehow banal.

A day or two later, Mr. Loath presided over his tutorial: the pasty, sweating, spotty boys, one other girl, and me. A small question of criminality was raised, and Mr. L. got testy: come along, come along, he said, do you know the maximum penalty under the Theft Act, do you, boy, or next boy, do you? I had to speak up and spare the boys from their humiliation; oh, Mr. Loath, I said, is it not ten years? Mr. Loath, fuming with frustration, was just about to snap the arm of his spectacles; his fingers relaxed, and "Thank goodness!" he said. And just as he replaced his glasses on his head, a pain sliced through me, diagonal, from my right ribs to my left loin. It was a new pain: but not new for long. It stole my life: it stole it for ten years and for a double term, and then for ten years more.

A short time later I was vomiting a good deal. I had finished the course of antidepressants, but felt no more cheerful, and my GP did what you do when someone says she is vomiting: send her to a psychiatrist. I should like to say I protested, but I was willing enough. I thought perhaps I was a fascinating case. I had been tested for anemia, but I wasn't iron deficient. No one seemed to be able to think of another disorder to test me for, and if my body was not the problem it must be my mind that was acting up; I could believe this, and wanted my mind fixed. "Psychosomatic" was the buzz word. Properly understood, the term suggests a subtle interaction between mind and body, between the brain and the endocrine system. Improperly understood, it means, "it's all in the mind"—that is to say, your symptoms are invented. You've nothing better to do with your time. You're seeking attention.

Dr. G., the psychiatrist, was remote and bald. He had as much chance of understanding a girl like me as he had of rising from his desk and skimming from the window on silver pinions. He soon diagnosed my problem: stress, caused by over-ambition. This was a female complaint, one which people believed in, in those years, just as the Greeks believed that women were made ill by their wombs cutting loose and wandering about their bodies. I had told Dr. G., in response to his questions about my family, that my mother was a fashion buyer in a large department store; it was true, for at the end of the sixties she had reinvented herself as a blond, bought herself some new clothes, and taken up a career. Oh really, said Dr. G.: how interesting. Thereafter, he referred to her place of work as "the dress shop." If I were honest with myself, he asked, wouldn't I rather have a job in my mother's dress shop than study law? Wouldn't the dress shop, when all's said and done, be more in my line?

I saw Dr. G. once a week. He must have obtained reports about me from my tutors, for he said, conscientious, hm, it says you're very conscientious.

Was I? I only turned in the work asked for. Didn't other people bother?

"And a mind for detail," Dr. G. said, "you have that." I tried to imagine the other kind of law student, the kind who favored the broad-brush approach, who took on the law of trusts, for example, with a grand generalist's sweep and dash. "Tell me," said Dr. G., "if you were a doctor, what kind would you be?"

I said politely that to be a psychiatrist must be interesting. No, pick something else, he said, something less close to home. I'd often thought, I said, that GPs had a challenging job, the variety of people and problems, the need for quick thinking—but no, I could see by his face that wasn't the answer required. Dr. G. sat back in his chair. I see you as a medical researcher, he said, one of those quiet invaluable people in the back room, unseen, industrious, unsung—a mind for detail, you see. And wasn't it the same, he asked, with law? If I did go on with my studies, wouldn't the niche for me be in a solicitor's office, conveying clients' houses—wasn't it just what people needed, at such a stressful time in their lives, to have the services of someone very conscientious, like me?

I could see her: a clerk very conscientious and quiet and dull, who wore snuff-colored garb and filed herself in a cabinet every night and whose narrow heart fluttered when anyone mentioned a flying freehold or an ancient right of way. But you're not looking at me, I thought. I was quite thin; nausea was wearing me away. I left G.'s consulting room and stood on the pavement to consider this new version of myself. I felt as if I had been dealt a dull blow, but I didn't know which part of me ached.

The next time I went to Dr. G.'s office I sat and wept. It was as if a dam had burst. I must have worked through a box of tissues, and no doubt it was his upset-girl ration for the whole month. Dr. G. spoke kindly to me; said gravely he had not known that things were so bad. I had better have some stronger pills. And maybe a spell in the university clinic? I trucked off there, with my textbooks. At least now my husband would be able to study in peace for his finals. I wasn't easy company; I was laboring under a violent sense of injustice that may have seemed unreasonable to the people around me; I was angry, tearful, and despairing, and I still had pains in my legs.

I think, in retrospect, that it would have been better if I had denied that I had pains in my legs, if I had taken it all back, or brightly said that I was well now. But because I didn't, the whole business began to spiral out of control. I still believed that honesty was the best policy; but the brute fact was, I was an invalid now, and I wasn't entitled to a policy, not a policy of my own. I feared that if I didn't tell the strict truth, my integrity would be eroded; I would have nothing then, no place to stand. The more I said that I had a physical illness, the more they said I had a mental illness. The more I questioned the nature, the reality of the mental illness, the more I was found to be in denial, deluded. I was confused; when I spoke of my confusion, my speech turned into a symptom. No one ventured a diagnosis: not out loud. It was in the nature of educated young women, it was believed, to be hysterical, neurotic, difficult, and out of control, and the object was to get them back under control, not by helping them examine their lives, or fix their practical problems—in my case, silverfish, sulking family, poverty, cold—but by giving them drugs which would make them indifferent to their mental pain—and in my case, indifferent to physical pain too.

The first line of medication, in those days, were the group of drugs called tricyclic antidepressants—which I had already sampled—and also what were then called "minor tranquilizers"; the pills marketed as Valium were the most famous example of the type. Highly popular in those days among overworked GPs, the minor tranquilizers are central-nervous-system depressants. They impair mental alertness and physical coordination. They dull anxiety. They are habit-forming and addictive.

The antidepressants didn't seem to be having much effect on me—or not the wanted effects, anyway, only the effects of making me unable to grapple with the written word, of making print slide sideways and fall out of the book. It didn't seem as if I would be able to sit my finals, Dr. G. said, but never mind: in view of my good work record, the university would grant me an aegrotat degree. Did I understand aegrotat? It meant "he was sick." I muttered "he, not she?" It would have been much healthier for me if I had stopped muttering, and kept smiling.

Valium, however, did work; it worked to damage me. Some people, given tranquilizers of this type, experience what is called a "paradoxical reaction." Instead of being soothed, they are enraged. One day I sat by the hearth at Roebuck Road and imagined myself starting fires—not in my own chimney, but fires in the houses of strangers, fires in the streets. Somewhere along the line, I seemed to have been damaged; I imagined myself doing damage, in my turn. I knew these thoughts were not rational, but I was obliged to entertain them; day by day I smoldered in a sullen fury, and when I saw a carving knife I looked at it with a new interest. I agreed to the clinic because I thought that, if I were to act on my impulses, someone would see me and stop me—before, at least, it got to arson and stabbing, and the deaths of strangers who had never harmed me at all.

After a day or two in the clinic I felt a little calmer. No one saw me as a danger; the danger was all in my own head. At first I came and went; I would go back to Roebuck Road during the day and do the cleaning. One day I went down to town to buy myself a nightdress. But because my vision was blurred, I misread the label, and came back with a size 16 instead of a size 10. "Look at this monster garment!" I cried gaily to the nurses; I was having one of my less murderous days, and trying to lighten the tone. "Look what I bought!"

My nightdress, I found, was viewed in a grave light. Why had I bought it? It was a mistake, I said, you see I . . . Didn't you hold it up? they asked me. Well, no, I, I just liked the pattern, I . . . Didn't you remember what size you were? Did you feel you didn't know? Yes, I know my size, but you see, my eyesight, it's misty, it's because of the drugs I . . . oh, never mind.

But they wouldn't drop the topic. It was obviously characteristic of mad girls to buy big nightdresses. Every time I spoke I dug myself into a deeper hole.

Dr. G. came to see me. Well, and what was I doing with myself now that I was free from my struggles with my textbooks? I have written a story, I offered brightly. It was a long story—that is to say, a short story, but long as these things go. Short but long, said Dr. G. Hm. And what was it about? A changeling, I said. A woman who believes her baby has been taken away, and a substitute provided in its place. I see, said Dr. G., and where and when did this occur? In rural Wales, I said, funnily enough. (I'd never been to Wales.) I don't have to say the date, but it feels like the early 1920s. I mean, judging by their furniture and clothes. Does it? said Dr. G. It's a time well before social insurance, anyway, I said. The doctor won't come up the mountain to see them because they can't pay. I see, said Dr. G. And how does it end? Oh, badly.

If you didn't respond to the first wave of drugs—if they didn't fix you, or you wouldn't take them—the possibility arose that you were not simply neurotic, hypochondriacal, and a bloody nuisance, but heading for a psychotic breakdown, for the badlands of schizophrenia, a career on a back ward. To head off this disaster, doctors would prescribe what were then called the major tranquilizers, a group of drugs intended to combat thought disorder and banish hallucinations and delusions.

The next time I saw Dr. G. he forbade me to write: or, more precisely, he said, "I don't want you writing." He put more energy into this statement than any I had heard him make. He seemed as remote as ever, and yet inexpressibly angry. "Because—" he added; and broke off. He was not going to impart to me what came after "because."

I said to myself, if I think of another story I will write it. In fact, I didn't think of another story for quite some years—not a story of the long but short type—and when I did I sent it to *Punch* and what I got back was not a malediction but a check. The changeling too paid off, in time, in a novel published in 1985; the setting was not rural Wales, nor the 1920s, but the present day in a prosperous and dull Midlands town. The novel contained mad people, but no one suggested its author was mad. It's different, somehow, when you've received money for your efforts; once you've got an agent, and professionalized the whole thing.

The first drug I was given was called Fentazine. That would do the job, Dr. G. thought.

Do you know about akathisia? It is a condition that develops as a side effect of antipsychotic medication, and the cunning thing about it is that it looks, and it feels, exactly like madness. The patient paces. She is unable to stay still. She wears a look of agitation and terror. She wrings her hands; she says she is in hell.

And from the inside, how does it feel? Akathisia is the worst thing I have ever experienced, the worst single, defined episode of my entire life—if I discount my meeting in the secret garden. No physical pain has ever matched that morning's uprush of killing fear, the hammering heart. You are impelled to move, to pace in a small room. You force yourself down into a chair, only to jump out of it. You choke; pressure rises inside your skull. Your hands pull at your clothing and tear at your arms. Your breathing becomes ragged. Your voice is like a bird's cry and your hands flutter like wings. You want to hurl yourself against the windows and the walls. Every fiber of your being is possessed by panic. Every moment endures for an age and yet you are transfixed by the present moment, stabbed by it; there is no sense of time passing, therefore no prospect of deliverance. A desperate feeling of urgency— a need to act—but to do what, and how?—throbs through your whole body, like the pulses of an electric shock.

You run out into the corridor. A man is standing there, gaz-ing dolefully toward you. It is your GP, the man at the Student Health Service, the man with the rimless glasses and the pol-ished brogues. The tension rises in your throat. Speech is dragged and jerked out of you, your ribs heaving. You think you are screaming but you are only whispering. You whisper that you are dying, you are damned, you are already being dipped into hell and you can feel the flames on your face.

And the answer to this? Another antipsychotic. An injection of Largactil knocked me into insensibility. I lay with my face in the pillow as the drug took effect, and sank into darkness; as I ceased to panic and fight, the hospital sheets dampened and wrapped around me like ropes.

After I woke up, I was maintained on Largactil, to combat my madness. It was not a friendly drug; it made my throat jump and close, as if someone were hanging me. This is how a mad person appears to the world—lips trembling, speech fumbling and jerky. You can say, this is the drugs you know, this is not me; I am quite all right, inside myself. They say, yes dear, of course you are; have you taken your pill?

But then it was the end of term, the end of the year. My course of studies was over. The university's responsibility was ended. I was discharged from the clinic. I went home, and was sane. The drugs wore off; I no longer twitched and jumped. I could have passed for normal in any company. My legs didn't seem to ache so much; I had more abdominal pain, but I knew better than to mention it. For a time I claimed to be well.

But it was not so easy to shake off the events of the last year. The problem was the names of those drugs I had "needed," spelled out like evil charms in my medical notes. Fentazine, Largactil, Stelazine. If I set foot in a GP's surgery—as I did, when I grew increasingly sick—I ran the risk of being prescribed a dose of them that would knock an elephant off its feet. Then there was my old friend Valium, which I knew I shouldn't go near: not unless I wanted to be arrested.

So when in time I went back to a doctor, I said I had backache, nausea, vomiting, that I was too tired to move. My GPs—to a man, and a woman—suggested a test to see if I was anemic. I never was. They had no other suggestions; except perhaps some Valium: and a little spell away might do me good? By the time I was twenty-four I had learned the hard way that whatever my mental distress—and it does distress one, to be ignored, invalidated, and humiliated—I must never, ever go near a psychiatrist or take a psychotropic drug. My vision blurred, in those days, entirely without the help of the antidepressants. Sometimes there were gaps in the world: I complained one day that the front door had been left open, but the truth was that I just couldn't see the door. Sometimes it seemed that some rustling, suspicious activity was going on, at the left side of my head, but I couldn't put a name to what it was. I couldn't put a name to lots of things, my speech came out muddled: I called a clock's hands its fingers, and a chair's arms its sleeves.

I was all right if I stuck with abstractions, ideas, images. And some days I was half-well. I had a job, but I needed a pursuit, I thought. I went to the library and got out a lot of books about the French Revolution. I made some notes and some charts. I went to a bigger library and got more books and began to break down the events of 1789–1794 so that I could put them into a card index. I was very conscientious and with a mind for detail. If you had been having a revolution you would certainly—at such a stressful time in your life—have needed the services of someone as conscientious as me. I began to read about the old régime, its casual cruelties, its heartless style. I thought, but I know this stuff. By nature, I knew about despotism: the unratified decisions, handed down from the top, arbitrarily enforced: the face of strength when it moves in on the weak.

One day, on a escalator in a department store, a man put a hand up my skirt. Enough, enough, I thought. I turned around and punched him in the eye. I got off at the top of the escalator and walked away.

I didn't like the world I was living in. It didn't seem too keen on me.

I was too sick to do a responsible job, a professional job. I got a job as a saleswoman, and I thumbed my nose at Dr. G.; I started to write a book. I wrote and wrote it. Time passed. I moved to another country, another continent. Still I wrote it and wrote it.

Christmas week 1979. I was twenty-seven years old. I was in St. George's Hospital in London having my fertility confiscated and my insides rearranged. When I was admitted, I knew I was very ill, but I didn't know quite how bad things might be, and for a time there was no agreement on the nature of what ailed me. Only that it was physical; only that I had a pain and it was real: only that it was a disease Valium wouldn't cure.

My life had moved on by then, far from its early confines. We had wanted to travel, to see the world; my husband had exchanged carboniferous limestone for the sands of the Kalahari, fossils for diamonds. For three years we had lived in a small town in Botswana, a railway line settlement, where geologists and agriculture specialists rumbled over the unmade roads in four-wheel drives, where ticks and mosquitoes bit, where the days were short and hot and monotonous, and I sat behind the insect mesh of my veranda frowning over my card index, documenting the fall of the French monarchy, the rise of the Committee of Public Safety. I had pressed the juice of meaning from every scrap of paper I had brought with me, every note on every source. The book was finished now. But so, it seemed, was I. When we came home to England on leave, my book went to a publisher who offered to look at it. I went to a consultant who offered to look at me.

In the beds around me were women with complications of pregnancy, who were trying to hang on to their babies; women having abortions; women having their fertility ended by choice. The latter group were two cheerful middle-aged women, a little worn and raddled by life, who complained at the routine discomforts, the marching up and down corridors and waiting in a draft to have blood samples taken; even their complaints were cheerful, and they really amounted to grumbling about the fact that for a couple of days they weren't in charge, because they were used to a situation where what they say, goes. They had taken this decision, they, for themselves: another baby, no thank you! They called the surgery "having my tubes tied"; I pictured the surgeon hauling ropes, shouting "heave-ho!" and consulting a book of knots. On my right there was a silent Turkish girl in her early twenties, having a termination which she was not, I suppose, discussing with her family; she wanted a cigarette, she said, just a little draw would soothe her. After the operation she appeared to have greenish-dark bruises around her eyes, as if someone had undertaken to knock sense into her. The bruises deepened to caverns, then lightened to a jaundiced tan. Then she was gone, discharged. When she climbed out of bed you saw her vitality, her dark bandy legs, her strength. She would have, you thought, just as many children as she liked.

Her fellow abortionee was opposite me, a tow-headed

sixteen-year-old on her second termination. We hopped from bed to bed, Kirsty and I, sitting each at the foot of the other. She told me about her life. She went out to dance and to shoplift a little and if anyone looked at the boy she happened to be with she would belt them around the head; isn't that right, she said, and we agreed that yes, it was the only thing to do. More perplexed than malicious, she called the nurses by whistling for them; she didn't understand their genteel nursy euphemisms, and when they handed her a flask and asked her to pass water she came across to ask if I knew what the fuck they were talking about.

Kirsty was taken to theater to have her termination; believing that she had no chance of looking after her body, of regulating her future fertility, the surgeon fitted an IUD while she was under anesthetic. But then the device fell out, one night when she was in the bathroom; she hemorrhaged, fainted with shock, and cracked her head open on the washbasin. Her life, you felt, would always be like this—the handing out of attrition, without regard to justice; fate would overreact to an ungoverned temper and the impulses of a generous heart. She had adopted me on my first day on the ward; I wasn't, she thought, getting my due. Until some time after I was admitted, the nurses could not manage to get a doctor up to the ward to organize pain relief for me. The strong pills I had brought with me were taken away, and I was given a Panadol, an over-the-counter remedy for everyday discomfort. A hot bath was promoted as the remedy for my pain; I laughed. That first night, I lay on the bed, my knees drawn up. Kirsty shouted at the nurses. "Look at her, look at her," she roared. "Give her sumfin." And they did—a rare opportunity—they told me it was my turn to push around the cocoa trolley. My turn, though I'd only just arrived! So I rolled off the bed and did it. "Cocoa? Horlicks?

Sugar with that?" I was not quite able to stand up straight: some inflamed growth inside me was bending me at the waist, pulling my abdomen, knotted with pain, down toward my knees. Silliness, I suspect, had set in; some endocrinological compassion-center was flooding my brain with substances that suggested nothing now mattered very much.

I had been admitted without any certain diagnosis. The professor in charge of gynecology had, in a civil way for which I remain grateful, found me a bed at short notice. Provided I didn't mind being in hospital for Christmas, he said, they could have me in about the twentieth and operate before the feast. I had felt bleak, on the journey down the motorway—not afraid, but feeling in a childish way that there was nothing to look forward to. After two Christmases in Africa, when I'd missed my family badly, this was not what I had planned. When the professor had examined me at Outpatients, a week or two earlier, I'd bled everywhere, onto his latex hands and the sheet beneath me. I thought he'd have been hardened to that, but he said, "I am afraid I am hurting you. I am sorry. I will stop now." I would have liked it if curiosity would have propelled him onward: pushing into the unseen, smoking meat of my body, and finding out its truth.

How can I write this, I wonder? I am a woman with a delicate mouth; I say nothing gross. I can write it, it seems; perhaps because I can pretend it is somebody else, bleeding on the table.

But at the time, I came to the vertical, sickly swaying. I mopped myself up and got into my clothes. I sat in a chair: black vinyl, splayed legs, the ridge of its back hard against my spine. You say you think it's endometriosis, he said. There's a good chance you're right. But he didn't look a happy man. Could it be anything else? I asked. How we conspire, not to speak the word "cancer." His eyes slid away. Oh well, he said, if not endometriosis, then pelvic inflammatory disease, it is a thing to consider. I said, no I don't think so really. He nodded. He didn't think so, either. He said by the way, is it, should I, am I speaking to Doctor McEwen? I looked up to see if he was being sarcastic. No, I said, I'm not a doctor, why would you think that? Only, he said, your terminology is precise. Ah well, I thought. If only you knew me: conscientious, with a mind for detail. Little Miss Neverwell had graduated at last.

Endometriosis is a gynecological condition with a dazzling variety of systemic effects. It is not rare, though mercifully it is rare for the disease to run on, unrecognized, for as long as it did in me, and it is rare for it to do such damage. Because of the number of symptoms it throws up it is sometimes hard to diagnose. It is always hard to diagnose, for a doctor who doesn't listen and doesn't look. It is comparatively easy if you are the patient, and get into your hands a good textbook with a comprehensive account of its effects.

A few months earlier—in the remoteness of my small town on the fringes of the bush—I had thought, once again: enough's enough. My doctor (his dusty downtown surgery darkened by eucalyptus trees) seemed disinclined to investigate, though happy to prescribe me stronger and stronger pain relief. Whatever he gave me (and however much alcohol I knocked back to accompany it), the pain grew over the top. So one day I went up to the capital, to the university library, and combed through the medical books. I found a textbook of surgery, with a female figure, her organs clearly depicted, and black lines—like the long pins with which they used to stick witches—striking through her hips and rib cage, carrying a name for each organ. For each organ, there was a pain, and of each pain, I had a sample.

I learned next how the disease process worked. The endometrium is the lining of the womb. It is made of special cells which shed each month by bleeding. In endometriosis, these cells are found in other parts of the body. (How they get there is a matter of dispute.) Typically, they are found in the pelvis, in the bladder, the bowel. More rarely, they are found in the chest wall, the heart, the head. Wherever they are found, they obey their essential nature and bleed. Scar tissue is formed, in the body's inner spaces and small cavities. It builds up. It presses on nerves and causes pain, sometimes at distant sites. The scar tissue forms an evil stitching which attaches one organ to another. Infertility is a distinct possibility, as the organs of the pelvis are ensnared and tugged out of shape. Endometriosis in the intestines makes you vomit and gives you pains in the gut. Pressure in the pelvis makes your back ache, your legs ache. You are too tired to move. The pain, which in the early stages invades you when you menstruate, begins to take over your whole month. Lately I had known days of my life when everything hurt, everything from my collar bone down to my knees. But hey! There was nothing wrong with my ankles. My feet were performing nicely. And I could still think, and depress the typewriter keys. Stop complaining! I thought. Look where complaining gets you! In the madhouse.

Along with endometriosis goes, not infrequently, a hormonal disarrangement which shows itself as a severe premenstrual syndrome. In my case, it manifested in the prodromal aura of migraine headaches. Migraine, I had to learn, was not just a sick headache. It was a series of linked neurological phenomena of remarkable diversity. It was within the migraine aura that my words came out wrong, that the door disappeared into a black space: it was within the aura that I heard the dull hum and the muttering on the left-hand side of my head.

Migraine stirred the air in dull shifts and eddies, charged it with invisible presences and the echoes of strangers' voices; it gave me morbid visions, like visitations, premonitions of dissolution. For a time, when I was eight years old, my field of vision was filled with a constant, moving backdrop of tiny skulls. As a student, I had told Dr. G. about them, in a burst of frightened confidence. "Black on a white ground, skulls skulls skulls, the size of my little fingernail, unrolling," I said. "Unrolling, like a satanist's wallpaper." Dr. G. smiled a wintery smile. "Ah well," he said. At this stage, I was only a neurotic, not the full-fledged madwoman I would become when he upped my dosage. "Ah well." His voice was soothing. "We all have our little metaphysical fancies."

Nineteen seventy-nine: I must admit that the very act of climbing into the hospital bed had brought me a kind of relief. I could stop pretending to be well. The odd thing, though, as I had already observed, was that the staff were inclined to treat the patients as malingerers. We could see them huddled at their nurses' station, flicking through our notes and discussing our body parts. Young girls with flaky cervixes were probably no better than they should be, and anything in the pelvic inflammatory line attested to a vibrant sex life. Pregnant women weren't sick, women wanting abortions weren't sick, and as for the sterilization brigade, they should probably be up and scrubbing the latrines. (That wouldn't have come amiss.) And as for me—I soon got a jolly diagnosis. The senior registrar examined me and thought I was pregnant. He winked at me. That's a baby in there, he said, confidently patting my swollen abdomen. He ran off to get a fetal heart monitor.

But there was no baby. Not Catriona, not Modestine: not anyone, only the ghost of my own heartbeat, amplified to the outside world. Oh well, the registrar said. Looks like I was wrong, eh?

The houseman came, to take a history. He was very new and young, with a starter mustache, which could be studied bristle by bristle; some bristles stuck out at a right angle to his skin. I kept my eye on it, and the movements of his mouth. You are very young, he said, and I am going to ask the professor, yes yes (he got up his resolve), I am going to talk to the professor, I am going to ask him if he can make a neat low incision, so that afterward, you will be able to wear a bikini. He looked almost tearful. I nodded. I knew he would not be able to effect this, but I liked it that he cared so much. It is strange, to expose your soft girlish body to a man of your own age, who has not yet acquired dispassion but wears a white coat. In fact, I said, I never wear a bikini because I am too—I wanted to say, modest. But what modesty was left? I'd had more gynecologists than I'd had lovers; alien fists in my guts. I said, you see, I am too white for a bikini. Too pale. I burn. Of course, he said. But all the same. He got up, flustered, his clipboard almost spilling his notes. At the bed's end, he turned and smiled, and winked at me.

Two days after I was admitted I needed to have an ultrasonic scan. For this I needed to cross London. St. George's Hospital at Hyde Park Corner was in its last weeks of occupation; it was gaunt, grubby, and nearly empty. My ward was almost the last to be kept open, I was told, and for the high-tech stuff I needed to go to the new St. George's at Tooting. I expected them to bring my clothes up the ward, but I was told, no, you have to go in your dressing gown, that's how patients go.

The only such garment I owned, myself, was a black satin wrap with a plunging neckline. But before I had been admitted to hospital my kind, practical cousin Beryl had said that she didn't think it would do, and lent me a green velour item, cozy and modest, that came to my ankles and buttoned up to the neck. I was very glad of it, when told I was to go by taxi to Tooting. They would organize the taxi, they said, no worries. Oh, I said to myself, I don't have to go out on the street and whistle for it? And, they said, they'd send someone to escort me.

Before I began the journey, I was to drink as much water as I could possibly bear to drink, to distend my bladder, which was a good thing for a reason nobody explained. In a way, you didn't want to ask. What if they didn't know? There was a trade-off in ignorance going on. They told me nothing, and I didn't ask questions in case I was shocked by finding how much they didn't know. I waited, sitting on my bed, pensively swigging from a hospital tumbler.

"Here's Della!" somebody shouted.

"Hello, hello!" Della shouted back. She rolled in like an Oscar candidate, like the belle of the ball. "Wha-ay, Della!" rose the shout. Della whooped back. I know a character, when I see one. And oh god, how a character shrinks my flesh with dread. I took one final sip of water.

Della was a Jamaican auxiliary, in her fifties or sixties. She was very wide, so that you felt you couldn't quite see around her. People must feel that about me, nowadays, but I don't think I block the light like Della did. She had a broad forehead and she glowered. She reminded me of a bison; not a bad thing, really, because as a child I liked the bisons at the zoo; they would stand near the fence, breathing bulkily, while you wormed your finger through the netting and scratched the expanse of sparse hair between their ears. But depend upon it: once on the open range, they could charge you down.

It was Della who was my promised escort to Tooting. They brought a wheelchair up to the ward. "To take you to the taxi," they said. But I said (maybe I just thought) I can walk, you know that, you make me walk, last night you invited me to operate the cocoa trolley . . . But they were insistent. They said it was a rule.

I was wheeled to the entrance and packed into a taxi with my bison. "Wotcha, Della!" said the porters at the main door (or some other vile mock-cockney exclamation). Della had, I suppose, been given a letter to hand to someone at the other end, but she didn't seem to know why we were going to Tooting together, regarding it with levity and as a kind of holiday treat. She hollered back to the porters, "Ray, what! Gwine Tootin, see yer, wot?"

The door slammed. We inched forward into the traffic of Hyde Park Corner. The driver kept his glass screen closed. But chat ran out of Della, chat chat chat. Who was I and why there, for what? I replied, a steady even flow of answers, censored against self-pity, censored against the personal, my face turning again and again to the taxi window. It took a long time, that journey, through the midday traffic, inching south, crossing the Thames. I have never come to terms with London as a city, but I like to look at it silently, from taxi windows, and appreciate it for what it is, and for how it makes me feel provincial. On this day I felt possessed by the idea that I might not see it again. Even two days in the enclosure of a hospital ward changes your vision, and the buildings to me seemed distant and heroic, like the buildings of a dream city. I felt emotional, but couldn't put a name to my emotion. My bladder, which had been attacked by the disease process, had swollen obediently, and already I had a pain: a new sort of pain, quite a change really. Della was talking, loosely, fluently. I was replying to everything she said. Then she began a new story. My mind rejoined her. She told me about her youngest daughter, only eighteen, who had gone into hospital five years ago to have an operation on her hand. "Just a little swellin'." Della insisted. "I told her, don't you bother about that. Would she listen? Would she listen? Ho no!"

I swiveled from the window. For much of the journey till now I hadn't known what Della was talking about, but surely this was something I could understand? And how did it go, I asked, for your daughter, did it work out all right, did they fix her up? Ho no! Della said. It all went wrong when they put her under. She's, like, a vegetable now. She got her brain destroyed. Vegetable's what they call it.

She spoke dispassionately, as if she were talking about a Martian. The law student in me was sick, but not entirely dead. In almost any circumstance, I would have leaned forward—conscientious, mind for detail—and said, you had a claim for negligence, did you get a good solicitor? I would have been slow to censure Della, for bringing up such a gloomy precedent, and considered that in fact she might have done me a favor: it gave me something other than my pains to think about. Did the hospital admit liability, and what damages did you get? Five years, I thought—five years, the case could still be enmeshed in the system. Only part of my mind flinched from what she had told me. The other part was about to ask her for the figures, for the dates. I was about to speak.

But then Della did a terrible thing. She let her head sag forward and her jowls hang, and she imitated her daughter's speech. "She goes, Ma, Ma, Ma. La, la, la. That's all she can do." Della protruded her tongue. She grunted. "Ma, ma, ma. La, la, la." She lolled her head on her thick neck. "Ma, ma, la, la." At length, after time for consideration, Della put her tongue back in.

We traveled the rest of the journey in silence. The taxi driver put us down at the wrong entrance. Della seemed to know where we ought to be, and we set off together, she with unclouded brow, as if rolling across the grassy plains, me in my dressing gown and bare feet in slippers: bending a little over my pain, as if I were brooding. I had come from the heat of Africa, at the hottest time of year, and we were in December. In fairness, I must say, it was neither raining nor snowing. It was one of those days so near the end of the year that it won't put the effort in: only a stray sullen flake drifted down, out of a sullen sky.

I had worked in a hospital, at one stage in my career, and understood medical signposts, so I wasn't happy with Della's choice of destination. But she insisted. She kept charging, her bison head down; I had to follow her. I wanted to crouch down, on the gravel path, and urinate beneath my skirts, like Marie Antoinette on the way to execution; it is a sad detail of that sad life, which in my manuscript about the Revolution I had thought long and hard about suppressing, but had not. Della led me to the liver unit, where people thirty years my senior were standing in line. They were waiting for scans, it was true, but special ones, peculiar to them. They were yellow, bloated people, who resembled each other, who seemed to have joined the same family. None of them spoke to me. They just looked. They were stooped, like me. They held their abdomens draped over their forearms, holding up their own swags of flesh: like debutantes scooping up their trains to nip out of Buckingham Palace after their presentation.

A nurse shook his head at Della. He pointed. We backed off, away from the yellow people. I looked into the moons of their faces and they looked back at me, tolerant, indifferent perhaps.

We set off again, me and Della, out of the liver unit and into the open air, up the gravel walks and down. The cold was raw and wet, like a salt bath. When I got to the right place, they were expecting me. Perhaps they had been expecting me for the last hour, but they didn't criticize. A technician, kindly but dispassionate, slicked jelly onto my abdomen. It reminded me of Swarfega, a product with which the men in my life degreased their hands after tampering with a car engine. Perhaps the hospital could fix me, with some plastic padding? The technician loomed above me and rolled me with a roller. Lifting my head, I saw the pictures on the screen. It didn't look sensible, it didn't look reasonable, and perhaps he didn't think so either. But he was helpful in pointing out the salient features. "Nice full bladder," he said, "I expect you can't wait to get rid of that." He showed me the blossoming growths around my ovaries. For the first and last time, I saw my womb, with two black strokes, like skilled calligraphy, marking it out: a neat diacritical mark in a language I would never learn to speak.

After the rolling was over, I was allowed to fall from the examination table, and urinate. When we got back to St. George's, after another hour in a taxi, Della lollopped out of the cab and I followed gingerly, setting my slippered feet on the pavement. The porters shouted "Whoa, Della! Whay-hay, ducks!" "Bin Tootin," she bawled. "That's our gel," the porters bawled back. They ran out a wheelchair and looked at me expectantly. I'm not getting in that, I said, don't be ridiculous; I've run halfway round south London in my dressing gown.

But you have to, they said, aghast. There's no two ways about it. We can't have you walking; what a notion! It's more than our job's worth.

Della was singing now, her attention elsewhere. Oh, if it's your jobs, I said. I wouldn't like to get you sacked. That's the way! they said. I sank into the wheelchair for the ride up to the ward.

As Christmas approached, the ward emptied. The cheerful women went home, sterilized, healed, still grumbling. A husband brought a suitcase for a young wife who had been caught in the early stages of cervical cancer—cured, she thought, she hoped. In bed she had looked like a ten-year-old boy, buttoned up inside a sensible warm top, her pale hair tousled, her sharp face peaky. Now when the bed curtain swept back she stood straight and slim in three-inch heels, her angles encased in careful, beautiful clothes, which fitted her so exactly that you knew they had been made, by or for her; the precise hemline, the loose wool coat with its calibrated swing. She shook her head, and her thick blond bob, precision-cut, settled into place, grazing her shoulder pads; she picked up her burnished leather bag, and stepped out into the rest of her life.

London emptied. The traffic stilled at Hyde Park Corner. A young woman remained in an opposite bed, six months pregnant, her face mottled with fever; she had a kidney infection and was, in the ward's parlance, "poorly." When the antibiotics began to work she sat up and looked about her with misty, Celtic eyes; her dark hair filmed the white pillow.

When the kidney girl sat up, it was already the eve of my surgery. No one had agreed yet on the nature of my problem. My husband had been told that, in the event that the growths were malignant, he should expect my death. I had not been given the message, but I didn't really need it. I stubbornly believed in my own diagnosis. If I was right, I would survive.

Many hours after dark, the carol singers came. I was in the bathroom at the time, standing with my back to the dark mirror. I had begun to feel, not afraid but very lonely; I had given way to self-pity, and tears were springing out of my eyes when they piped up with "Once in Royal David's City." I stood till it was over, leaning against the wall. Then I heard a woman say, in a sweet bossy voice, "Perhaps you would care to choose a carol, dear?" And Kirsty laughed: a long peal, like glad tidings. They had swooped on Kirsty because she was in the first bed they came to; they had handed her a hymn book, and when I shot out of the bathroom she was holding it as if it were hot, and her laughter was the sound of her incredulity. I took the book from her; she darted a grateful glance. I flicked the pages over, and asked for "God Rest You Merry, Gentlemen." The singers complied, though they looked a bit disappointed at such an old-fashioned choice. But I was thinking of our surgeons, coming tomorrow to cut me up; it was the last thing they would do, before going home to their families to carve the Christmas fowl.

After the singers had gone Kirsty fell into a dead sleep. I sat on the end of the kidney girl's bed and we smoked a cigarette. "Ladies, back to bed!" the staff cried. I was the only one up, but they made me plural because they didn't care to confront me. Eventually I kissed the kidney girl goodnight, stroking back her dark hair; there was no one else to do it. I shuffled across to my own bed and edged myself beneath the covers. The mound of my abdomen was almost as big as kidney girl's pregnancy, and they still hadn't sorted out pain relief. They gave me a sleeping pill, but it would have taken a mallet to knock me out. I was not afraid, but my brain was active.

In the silence of the night, toward two o'clock, came an African woman in trouble, rocking her head from side to side, on a stretcher which had taken on the aspect of a bier. Two men, their faces stricken, walked behind her. The cold had given them an ashy hue, and they carried woolen hats, which they wrung between their hands.

I was brought up as a Christian, in so far as a Catholic may be so called. (My grandmother thought you didn't want to be reading the Bible, she thought it was a Protestant book.) Christians are given, for their psychic support, the model of a man dying in extreme agony. As Catholics we were encouraged in my childhood to follow the "Stations of the Cross," praying certain prayers at each depiction of the stages of Christ's Passion. We were taught to be thankful that, whatever was in store for us, it wasn't crucifixion: unless we were a missionary or really unlucky.

As a Catholic, you were taught to contemplate your last end. You were encouraged to rehearse, in advance, your own death: with its accompanying agonies of mind and body, and (I found this a homely touch) your friends and relations hovering about your bed.

It is true that the "Litany for a Happy Death" didn't form part of the prayers I was taught in school. But at eight or nine years old, bored with the unvarying form of Holy Mass, and in despair of hearing a good sermon, I used to thumb through to the back of the prayer book.

"O Lord Jesus, God of goodness and Father of mercies, I draw nigh to thee with a contrite and humble heart; to Thee I recommend the last hour of my life, and that judgement which awaits me afterwards."

"When my feet, benumbed with death, shall admonish me that my mortal course is drawing to an end, Merciful Jesus, have mercy on me."

"When my hands, cold and trembling, shall no longer be able to clasp the crucifix, and, against my will shall let it fall on my bed of suffering, Merciful Jesus, have mercy on me."

"When my eyes, dim and troubled at the approach of death, shall fix themselves on Thee, my last and only support, Merciful Jesus, have mercy on me."

"When my lips, pale and trembling, shall pronounce for the last time Thine adorable name, Merciful Jesus, have mercy on me."

I take death as serious and proximate, I always have. But recently, when a doctor asked for my family history, I had to knock him back on every score. No heart disease. No strokes. No cancer: except for Grandad, and he was a smoker. No reason, in fact (I said this wonderingly, raising my face), no reason, it seems, we should ever die.

But the litany tells us we will, and how it will look:

"When my face, pale and livid, shall inspire the beholders with pity and dismay; when my hair, bathed in the sweat of death, and stiffening on my head, shall forebode my approaching end, Merciful Jesus, have mercy on me."

"When mine ears, soon to be forever shut to the discourse of men, shall be open to hear the irrevocable decree, which is to fix my doom for all eternity, Merciful Jesus, have mercy on me."

"When my imagination, agitated by dreadful specters—" but no, perhaps I have agitated you enough. I admire particularly the phrase about the hair stiffening on the head. This road to dissolution, the good Catholic was encouraged to walk regularly, following Christ to Calvary. Saint Peter, we were taught, was crucified upside down; this was more merciful for him, since he would have lost consciousness. I was told this three times during my high-school education, by the same woman, and each time in my mind I rehearsed her solemn upending, as if she were a geometrical figure that I had been asked to envisage in some other position. I think she believed Peter had got off lightly.

"When the last tear, the forerunner of my dissolution, shall drop from mine eyes, receive it as a sacrifice of expiation for my sins; grant that I may expire the victim of penance, and in that dreadful moment, Merciful Jesus, have mercy on me."

Note that excellent semicolon. People ask how I learned to write. That's where I learned it.

The whole of a Catholic life is lived in the shadow of the happy death—as if your life were to be enacted through a silvered, speckled mirror, ancient and flattering.

La la la. Ma ma ma. December 1979: I felt the urge to leave a note by my bed: if I wake up a vegetable, put me in a stew.

When I was half-awake, a day later, they came to tell me what they had done. After a general anesthetic, you dip in and out of consciousness: sitting up and smiling, you may be the picture of alertness, but your attention has faded. They should have told me again, I think, when I was properly awake. They should have told me once or twice. They should have written me a letter, they should have written me an essay or maybe a small book.

Certain things were over for me now. I sensed it would not be easy to shore up my collapsing marriage. When women apes have their wombs removed, and are returned by keepers to the community, their mates sense it, and desert them. It is a fact of base biology; there is little kindness in the animal kingdom, and I had been down there with the animals, grunting and bleeding on the porter's trolley. There would be no daughter, no Catriona; not that I could claim I had wanted her too hard; at twenty-seven I hadn't ever tried to have a baby. We seemed fine as we were, the two of us. "The children of lovers are orphans," said Robert Louis Stevenson. That would have been a sad fate for her, little Miss Cat. She would never be born now, and we were no longer lovers.

I was missing a few bits of me, besides my womb and ovaries, my reproductive apparatus. A few lengths of bowel: but you've plenty to spare.

Do you know what worries me most about this memoir? That I'm always the smart one. Always the one with the last word. Always the one with the heartless quip, the derisive bon mot.

But now I had to reckon with this: I hadn't been smart at all. Like a cretin, like some dumb little angel, I had believed what I was told. I believed that the pains which ran through my body each month were part of the burden of womanhood. I didn't say to my doctors, by the way, my menstrual periods are agony. I thought they would say, get away, you, little Miss Neverwell! And when I had, timidly, approached the topic, they'd said robustly, whoah, now, you don't want to worry! Period pains? That'll clear up, my dear, after you have your first baby. Just you wait and see!

I was brought up as a Catholic and it's not easy to throw over the faith. I believed that, short of crucifixion, you shouldn't really complain.

I was quickly out of bed. I tried to persuade the surgeons to let me go early, but they wouldn't. One of the girls on the ward had got a makeup kit for Christmas, and told me to help myself to it. I thought we should have our faces on, to meet 1980, so though I wasn't very upright, because of my stitches, I painted us, young and old. Even Elsie, who was eighty-three, blushed beneath her blusher when I held up the hand mirror so she could see my work. "Look at me," she said, "Is that me? I've never worn rouge!"

For the rest of us, I painted deep kohl eyes, and ruby lips. The senior registrar came in, and caught me crouching over my patient. "Oh, you girls," he said, laughing. He walked away, chuckling to himself: another bunch of happy punters.

Oh, you girls! What are you like?

The incision ran up the midline of my body, slashed from pubic bone to navel.

About four months later, after repeated courses of penicillin had got me over the infections that I had contracted while in the hospital, I returned to Botswana, to my ailing marriage, my house, my dogs and cats. I am going to be better now, I said, I am going to be different. I went back to the GP who had been treating me, or failing to treat me: downtown, the dusty consulting room under the eucalyptus trees. I found it hard to talk; I thought I had nothing to be ashamed of, but somehow I felt ashamed, and I was not sure how confidential was my consultation; secrets did seem to leak, in this small bush town. I told him about the surgery, shuffling my feet. "So," I said, "you see, in the end, it turned out there wasn't much to be done, by the stage I'd reached. It turned out a bit of a catastrophe."

"Oh well," he said. He shuffled his own sandaled feet under his desk. "There's one good thing, anyway. Now you won't have to worry about birth prevention."

I had been, until Christmas, a woman who thought she had a choice. I was twenty-seven and I thought I could have a baby, even if I didn't want one, even if my husband didn't; I was free in the matter, there were possibilities. Now I was not free and

the possibilities were closed off. Biology was destiny. Neglect—
my own, and that of the medical profession—had taken away
my choices. Now my body was not my own. It was a thing
done to, a thing operated on. I was twenty-seven and an old
woman, all at once. I had undergone what is called a "surgical
menopause" or what textbooks of the time called "female castration." I was a eunuch, then? Castration is a punishment; what
was my crime? It used to be fashionable to call endometriosis
"the career woman's disease": the implication being, there now,
you callous bitch, see what you get if you put off breeding and
put your own ambitions first. I was no good for breeding, so
what was I good for? Who was I at all? My hormonal circuits
were busted, my endocrinology was shot to pieces. I was old
while I was young, I was an ape, I was a blot on the page, I was
a nothing, zilch. The publisher had turned down my French
Revolution book. It seemed I couldn't even write. But come
now—let's break open the champagne! At least I won't have to
worry about birth prevention!

There are times in life when you are justified in punching
someone in the face. But I didn't react. I knew it was for the
doctor to direct the blow, and me to absorb it. Sometimes one
takes a little pride in endurance of this kind. At that stage, it
was all that was left.

When I left St. George's Hospital, I imagined that aspects of
my past had been excised, cut cleanly away. My long scar
would knit and the memory of the pain would fade. For a time
I went to and fro, between England and Africa, and in the end
I tried to put down roots in the colder climate, and make my
way alone. But by 1982 I was sick again, pain slicing through
my vital organs and leaving me breathless in public places,

leaning against a grimy wall at Euston Station, or clinging like a derelict to a park bench. My skin turned gray, and my weight began to fall, so that one day, when I saw myself sideways through a mirror, I shocked myself: I looked like one of those beaten dogs that the RSPCA used to photograph, with bones sticking through the hide. I hadn't known that the endometriosis could come back.

Though it is true that radical surgery is usually a cure for the condition, it is also the case that it is difficult to eradicate every misplaced cell, to pick off those minute guerrilla fighters waging a long war in the obscure cavities of the body. The hormone estrogen, like fresh supplies and matériel, allows the guerrillas to flourish. I didn't know that then. If I didn't take estrogen replacement, I had been told, my bones would crumble. How much to take? No one seemed to know. Trial and error, I was told breezily. Take enough so that you don't get the symptoms of the menopause.

Soon I was suffering almost continuous pain. Ignorant doctors whom I encountered told me the disease could not return. The pain was the pull of scar tissue, adhesions, or if it wasn't that, then once again I was imagining things. This should have made me angry, but I was too fragile and worn to react as I should. There was little information available to the public, no support groups in those days. When I found a doctor who believed in my problem and was prepared to treat me, my reaction was only gratitude.

The treatment was drugs now, hormones. The first weeks were tough. On a summer's day, wrapped in a big quilt, my teeth chattered as they had in Africa when I had contracted dysentery. But the tropical infection had left me light and hollow; now, I seemed to be gaining flesh. I entered treatment weighing something over seven and a half stone. By the end of nine months, which was the usual duration of the course, the pain was no better, but my bodyweight had increased by over 50 percent and was rising.

When I gained the first stone or two, I didn't really mind. If you are secure in one aspect of your appearance—and there had never been anything to quibble about, with my shape—you don't mind small changes, they don't seem threatening, and in fact they give you a chance to alter your style. I'd always been afraid of showing my arms, in case people thought I was from the Third World and gave me a donation; and my upper ribs, I'd always thought, looked somewhat tubercular. It was good that I looked healthier; I was tired of people asking what was wrong with me, and giving me those dirty looks that very thin women get all the time. I'd even been turned down for a job, by a broad-beamed horse-faced woman who said I looked weak: other jobs had been barred to me as soon as my medical record was discovered. It was a bit like going back to the 1970s. In those days, interviewers looked sourly at me because I was married, and looked fertile; so why didn't they like me any better, now I was on my own and incapable of childbearing?

At nine stone and size 12, graceful and curvaceous, I got a job. It was quite a menial one, so I got another, for the evenings. One job was in a shop, the other in a bar. The jobs needed a sort of uniform, so I bought some cheap black skirts and white tops. Within a couple of weeks I had grown out of them. My face was round and looked childish; I was becoming like some phenomenal baby, who astounds her attendants. When my next appointment with my consultant came, I said, I'm worried because I'm putting on weight so fast. She shot me a spiteful glance, from amid her own jowly folds. Now, she said, you know what it's like for the rest of us.

I found a secondhand shop quite near where I lived; it sold cast-offs from the bored, with the odd designer label. I was determined not to panic, but I stopped eating, of course; what else could I do? In any case, my body was staging some kind of revolt; colic, nausea, an inability to keep food inside me. To get out of the house for eight, I had to get up at six. I spent my scarce free time getting my hair done, lifted and teased and curled into a mane, so that I didn't look as if I had a pinhead on top of my sweetly plump shoulders. I was a size 14 for a while, and people would say, "You look so well—been away somewhere nice, have you?"

My ex-husband came back from Africa. He had once told me that I was so vain of my waistline that I would starve rather than gain an inch. But how did he know? In the past it had never been an issue. Now I had starved, and still gained five. Not to worry! He took me shopping. I bought some English-women's dresses, the pretty, floppy kind that go with creamy skin and broad haunches. We got married again. I had warned him by letter that I was fat now, but I knew I was being melo-dramatic. Size 14's not fat, not really, it's just—it's well. That's what it is. Well.

I never was a size 16. I shot past it effortlessly. Soon there was nothing in the secondhand shop to fit me; bigger women don't discard fashions so lightly. The assistants—and hadn't I been their best customer all summer?—began to give me the smirk, half commiserating and half condescending, that would soon become the usual expression of shop girls when I went to get clad. My skin turned gray, shading to slate blue as the autumn came on. My legs swelled and ached. Fluid puffed up my eyelids. Some mornings my head looked like a soccer ball. I was glad when my husband's job took us to Saudi Arabia, where women wear drapery rather than clothes, and where no one knew me, so that no one could stop me in the street to say how well I looked; where, in fact, I was more or less prohibited from going out on the street at all. I could stay indoors, under artificial light, waxing like some strange fungus.

The failure of my drugs had been recognized, and before I left England I was put on a new type. By now I was not so green in judgment. I looked up the side effects. Weight gain—I'd done that, and I didn't think there were sizes bigger than 20: not really, not for people who'd once been thin. Hair falls out. Well, I had plenty of hair. Voice deepens—never mind, I'd always been a squeaker. Spots—harder to put a good face on spots, but never mind, the clued-up woman knows how to cope with a little outbreak. A general virilization . . . oh, what's the odds? I'd always wanted to be a bloke.

A few weeks on, I had developed a steroid moon-face. My hair had come out in handfuls. I was deaf, my eyesight was blurred by constant headaches, and my legs were swollen like bolsters. And one morning I sat up in bed, and cried out, like a nude exposed in a comic strip, Eek! I clapped my outstretched palms where my breasts had been, and there they weren't anymore.

Then I had a bit of luck. I needed a prescription, and a doctor's letter; my new drugs would have to be sent for from England, as they were not available in Saudi Arabia. I swayed, giddy and wincing, into a doctor's office. Let me name him—why not? His name was Dr. Fishlock. He sat up at the sight of me, and asked, "What are you taking?" He fixed me with a keen look, of knowledge and concern. I told him. It confirmed what he had suspected. He knew the drug, he said. He had worked on the clinical trials. It was effective: but but but.

I knew the buts. I was a walking but. A butt of ridicule, in my own eyes; a sad sack enclosing a disease process, no longer an object of respect, or self-respect. He spoke to me kindly, and cut the dose by a third.

Very few doctors understand this: that somehow, you have to live till you're cured.

I went home, to the dark, enclosed rooms of our city apartment. I cut my dose by a third. Bald, odd-shaped, deaf but not defeated, I sat down and wrote another book.

When I was thin I had no notion of what being fat is like. When I worked in a department store I had sold clothes to women of most sizes, so I should have known; but perhaps you have to experience the state from the inside, to understand what fat is like. When you sell clothes you get very good at sizing people, but I had sized my customers as if they were fridge-freezers, or some other unnegotiable object, solid and with a height, width, and depth. Fat is not like this. It is insidious and creepy. It is not a matter of chest-waist-hip measurement. You get fat knees, fat feet, fat in bits of you that you'd never thought of. You get in a panic, and believe in strange diets; you give up carbohydrate, then fat, then you subsist for a bit on breakfast cereal and fruit because it seems easier that way; then you find yourself weak at the fat knees, at risk of falling over in the street. You get up on winter mornings to pack ice cubes into a diet shake that tastes like some imbibed jelly, a primitive life-form that will bud inside you. You throw tantrums in fat-lady shops, where the stock is grimy tat tacked together from cheap man-made fabric, choice of electric blue or cerise. You can't get your legs into boots, or your feet into last year's shoes.

You say, okay, then I'll be fat. As it seems you have no choice, you generously concur. But you become a little wary of adverbs like "generously." Of adjectives like "full-bodied," "womanly," or "ample." You think people are staring at you, talking about you. They probably are. One of my favored grim sports, since I became a published writer and had people to interview me, has been to wait and see how the profiler will turn me out in print. With what adjective will they characterize the startlingly round woman on whose sofa they are lolling? "Apple-cheeked," is the sweetest. "Maternal" made me smile: well, almost.

Okay, you say, it seems I can't be thin, so I'll be fat and make the best of it. "Fat is a Feminist Issue," you tell yourself. Fat is not immoral. There is no link between your waistline and your ethics. But though you insist on this, in your own mind, everything tells you you're wrong: or let's say, you're going in for a form of intellectual discrimination that cuts against the perception of most of the population, who know that overweight people are lazy, undisciplined slobs. Their perception, of course, is conditioned, not natural. The ancient prejudice in favor of fat has reversed only recently. When I taught in African schools, the high-school girls thought slimness was a prize to be gained by hard study. As soon as their certificates allowed them to get away from mealie porridge, the diet of their foremothers, they planned to turn svelte. But poor girls, without certificates, who I met at my volunteer project, were aiming only to get as much mealie porridge as the high-school students. "Tell me about your best friend," I urged my little maids one day. "Now, write it down. Two sentences, can you?" My star pupil leaned against me, in friendly local style, while she read her composition. Her exercise book flopped in my lap, one sinewy arm was thrown across my shoulders. Her other hand trailed toward the book, her finger stabbed at the words: "My beast friend is Neo. It is a beautiful girl, and fat."

I think of her sometimes, my beast friend. In the terms of the church in which I was brought up, the body is a beast, a base, simian relative that turns up at the door of the spirit too often for comfort; a bawling uncle, drunk, who raps with the door knocker and sings in the street. Saints starve. They diet till they see visions. Sometimes they see the towers of the fortresses of God, the battlements outlined in flickering light. They are haunted by strange odors: heavenly perfumes, or diabolic stenches. Sometimes they have to rise from their pallets and kick their demons out. Some saints are muscular Christians. But there are no fat saints.

When you get fat, you get a new personality. You can't help it. Complete strangers ascribe it to you. When I was thin and quick on my feet, a girl with a head of blond hair, I went for weeks without a kind word. But why would I need one? When I grew fat, I was assumed to be placid. I was the same strung-out fired-up person I'd always been, but to the outward eye I had acquired serenity. A whole range of maternal virtues were ascribed to me. I was (and am) unsure about how I am related to my old self, or to myself from year to year. The hormonal profile of an individual determines much of the manifest personality. If you skew the endocrine system, you lose the pathways to self. When endocrine patterns change it alters the way you think and feel. One shift in the pattern tends to trip another.

Sometime about the millennium, I stopped being able to think properly. I lost my capacity for snappy summation, and my sense of priorities went too, so that when I was writing I would dwell on minor points at great length, while failing to get around to the main point at all. I could start things, but not finish them. I had no appetite, but grew still wider. Sleep became my only interest. In the end, it was discovered that my thyroid gland had failed. A simple pill treats it; your brain works again, but your body is slower to catch up. Nowadays, more than twenty years on from my trip to St. George's Hospital, everything about me—my physiology, my psychology, feels constantly under assault: I am a shabby old building in an area of heavy shelling, which the inhabitants have vacated years ago.

I am not writing to solicit any special sympathy. People survive much worse and never put pen to paper. I am writing in order to take charge of the story of my childhood and my childlessness; and in order to locate myself, if not within a body, then in the narrow space between one letter and the next, between the lines where the ghosts of meaning are. Spirit needs a house and lodges where it can; you don't kill yourself, just because you need loose covers rather than frocks. There are other people who, like me, have had the roots of their personality torn up. You need to find yourself, in the maze of social expectation, the thickets of memory: just which bits of you are left intact? I have been so mauled by medical procedures, so sabotaged and made over, so thin and so fat, that sometimes I feel that each morning it is necessary to write myself into being—even if the writing is aimless doodling that no one will ever read, or the diary that no one can see till I'm dead. When you have committed enough words to paper you feel you have a spine stiff enough to stand up in the wind. But when you stop writing you find that's all you are, a spine, a row of rattling vertebrae, dried out like an old quill pen.

When you were a child you had to create yourself from whatever was to hand. You had to construct yourself and make yourself into a person, fitting somehow into the niche that in your family has been always vacant, or into a vacancy left by someone dead; sometimes you looked toward dead man's shoes, seeing how, in time, you would replace your grandmother, or her elder sister, or someone who no one really remembered but who ought to have been there: someone's miscarriage, someone's dead child. Much of what happened to you, in your early life, was constructed inside your head. You were a passive observer, you were the done-to, you were the not-explained-to; you had to listen at doors for information, or sometimes it was what you overheard; but just as often it was disinformation, or half a tale, and much of the time you probably put the wrong construction on what you picked up. How then can you create a narrative of your own life? Janet Frame compares the process to finding a bunch of old rags, and trying to make a dress. A party dress, I'd say: something fit to be seen in. Something to go out in and face the world.

For a few years, in my dreams, I stayed thin, and I wore a thin person's clothes. Even today, I sometimes see myself, in one of the cities I go to when I am asleep, coming out of a bookshop or sitting at a café table, trim and narrow, though younger than I am now. It is said that, in dreams—in a lucid dream, where you are aware of your own processes—you can't turn on an electric light, or see yourself in a mirror. I set myself to test this; thinking that somehow, if I could see my fat self in a dream, I would have accepted it all through, and would accept the waking reality.

But what happens, when you face the mirror, is that its surface melts, and the self walks into the glass. You step through it, and into a different dream.

It was 1982 when I went to Saudi Arabia; I was thirty. The expatriate wives of Jeddah plagued the life out of me, sticking me like mosquitoes with their common question: "When are you going to start your family?"

I didn't know what was a good answer to this: I'm not, or I can't.

When I was a young woman I didn't want children. I was wary of the trap that seemed ready to spring. I was ambitious, on my own account, to make a mark on the world. I didn't want to carry someone else's thwarted expectations. If I failed to make something of myself, wouldn't I heap my frustration onto my daughter? And she, in course of time, onto her daughter? When is it a woman's turn, I wanted to know, to get something for herself, and not at second hand through her children? I was good for more than breeding: that was my opinion.

But my opinion faltered, in the face of the expat matrons smelling so sweetly of baby talc and cream. It was hard to tell them that I had turned my back on everything that gave life meaning for them, turned my back until it was too late for me. Once it was necessary for my husband's employer to arrange for my drugs to be brought in by courier, the rumor got about that they were fertility drugs. "They can do wonders nowadays," I was assured. Eyes were on my waistline; which was, of course, ever-expanding. After the natural gestation period had passed, the ladies gossiped among themselves that I was trying to adopt.

This made me angry; after a bit, it made me laugh. Would any agency have thought me a suitable adoptive mother? Adoption agencies don't like sick women for parents. And why would I want a child not my own? I needed to reflect my glorious ancestry. My forebear who crushed a riot, who was made a sanitary inspector. My great-grandmother, who liked a drink but never smoked a pipe. My great-grandfather, who built a wall an army could have marched on.

I should have been a "schoolgirl mother," I thought: that social scourge. At fourteen I might have been fertile. At seventeen. But after that—I have to read my pain backward, to know what was happening inside me—I guess my chances were decreasing. Those crippling spasms that had to be ignored, those deep aches with no name, those washes of nausea, were not evidence of a neurotic personality, or of my ambivalence about my gender, and they were not brought on by "nerves," or by fear of failure in a man's world. They were evidence of a pathological process that would destroy the chance of my having a child and land me with chronic ill-health. I wonder why, despite all, I did not insist, could not insist, that doctors paid attention to me and located my malaise. There are several possible explanations, on several levels. One is that, in the time and place where I grew up, expectations of health were low, especially for women. The proper attitude to doctors was humble gratitude; you cleaned the house before they arrived. The deeper explanation is that I always felt that I deserved very little, that I would probably not be happy in life, and that the safest thing was to lie down and die. The reasons for this elude me now. I wish I could explain them better, and make them add up. But we were always told at school, when tackling a sum, to "show your workings." Even if you didn't get the answer right, we were told, you might get the odd mark for honest effort.

What I would have liked was a choice in life. Leisure, to reverse my earlier decision that children didn't matter to me; leisure, to ask if circumstances or my mind had changed. No one can predict that the game will be over for them at the age of twenty-seven. The time I fell in love is the time I should have acted, and now that an era of my life is over, and my schoolfriends are becoming grandmothers, I miss the child I never had. I know what Catriona would have been like. I have a mental picture of her, which I have built like one of those criminal profilers whose formulations—let's be honest—never fit too well. She would be nothing like me at all. She would be strong like my mother, broad-shouldered like my husband, with that milky Irish skin that freckles but never tans. I see her small competent hands, chopping an onion; making unwritten dishes, which she has never been taught to make. She would manage her money well, and perhaps manage other people's; perhaps that's how she'd make a living. She would drive a car, and sing in tune, and know about things like making curtains, which have always defeated me.

People romance about their children long before they are born—long before, and long after. They name them and rename them. They see them as their second chances, "a chance to get it right this time," as if they were able to give birth to themselves. They have children to compensate themselves for the things they didn't do or didn't get in their own early life. They conceive because they feel impelled to make up, to a nonexistent person, for a loss they themselves have suffered. Children are born because their parents feel the defects in themselves, and want to mend them; or because they are bored; or because they feel that in some mysterious way it is time for children, and that if they don't have them their selves will begin to leak meaning away. Some women have babies to give a present to their own mother, or to prove themselves her equal. Motives are seldom simple and never pure. Children are never simply themselves, coextensive with their own bodies, becoming alive to us when they turn in the womb, or with their first unaided breath. Their lives start long before birth, long before conception, and if they are aborted or miscarried or simply fail to materialize at all, they become ghosts within our lives.

Women who have miscarried know this, of course, but so

does any woman who has ever suspected herself to be pregnant when she wasn't. It's impossible not to calculate, if I had been—it would have been born, let's see, in November, ice on the roads, early dark; it would have been the offspring of late March, a child of uncertain sun and squalls. There are ghosts within the lives of men; a man with daughters brings his son into being through wishing him, as a man somehow better than himself, and a father of sons wraps his unborn daughter in swaddling bands and guards her virginity, like an unspoiled realm of himself. Even adulterers have their ghost children. Illicit lovers say: what would our child be like? Then, when they have parted or are forced apart, the child goes on growing up, a shadow, a half-shadow of possibility. The country of the unborn is crisscrossed by the roads not taken, the paths we turned our back on. In a sly state of half-becoming, they lurk in the shadowland of chances missed.

I never saw a ghost in Africa, though more than once death came so near me I had to grapple with him. It seemed to me that ghosts—the knocking, echoing, pesky sort—were a manifestation of Europe that would trail after the person who was not yet at home in Africa: who was only half-adjusted to a new, deeper state of emergency. I never felt that unease in the empty house, the queasiness of populated rooms where you can't see the population: or fear of the dark. It seemed to me that symbols in Africa organized themselves differently. Outward manifestation of inner chaos came in fatal road accidents and suicides: the truck without lights, the one drink too many, the misspelled police report that got filed in the waste bin. Any number of lives were trashed, casually, born and unborn; and in Africa, I actually knew a woman who died in childbirth. She was just one among the continent's casualties, but the one I used to speak to every day. I didn't like her much, in fact: I'd like to say I mourned, but it would be stretching a point.

Jeddah was different. My life in Saudi Arabia, for at least two years, was like life in jail. Simple force of will—or the force of simple will—could move the furniture and rip off the wardrobe doors. At times of stress, or on the brink of change, you can seem to act as a conduit for whatever disorganized, irrational forces are in the air. Shut in those dark rooms, life going on elsewhere, my body subject to strange mutations, I accumulated an anger that would rip a roof off.

When I came back to England, and gave up my concealing Islamic draperies, neighborly eyes would note my bulk and ask, when is your baby due? Sometimes kindly women, waiting on a station bench, would edge along for me. Once, a young Scots boy, too new to London to have lost his natural grace, offered me his seat on the tube, and because I felt so ill, I thanked him with an astonished smile, and sat on it. The unborn, whether they're named or not, whether or not they're acknowledged, have a way of insisting: a way of making their presence felt. No advance in medical technology was going to produce Catriona; she was lost. But when biological destiny veers from the norm, there are parts of the psyche that take time to catch up. You understand what has happened, the medical disaster; you reason about it. But there are layers of realization, and a feeling of loss takes time to sink through those layers. The body is not logical; it knows its own mad pathways. Mourning is not quick; when there is no body to bury, mourning is not final. I used to say (because flippancy was my weapon), look, it's a good thing I never had children, because I'd be putting them outside the door while I finished a paragraph: I'd be saying, don't you know I've this piece to do for the newspaper, why don't you go and play in the road? No more somber enemy of good art than the pram in the hall: did Connolly ever write a truer word?

But at a less conscious level, I kept on planning for Catriona: for her brothers, and for their children too. This is the only conclusion I can reach, when I look at the strange decisions I took about real estate in the late eighties, the nineties. Property was a sound investment, of course, but I think I had investments that went beyond the financial. The larders were stocked with food, the presses with sheets. We could have provisioned a small army from the stuff that was stacked in the garages. After we bought Owl Cottage, we had accumulated a total of seven bedrooms, four lavatories, a duplication of domestic machines, the capacity to wash clothes for eight people at once, to do the dishes for sixteen. Who did I think was coming, unless the unborn; or possibly the dead? The hungry family of uncles, wanting ham and Cheshire cheese: their own dead offspring, that missing generation: my own missing daughter trailing her offspring, a green-eyed girl with my green-eyed grandchildren. What's to be done with the lost, the dead, but write them into being?

There is a certain pathos attached to ghosts, to household sprites and those hobgoblins that jump into the vision between waking and sleep. At one time, I was plagued by a spate of dreams in which I was a midwife who had let a child die; but when I got my first book on track again, and when, after many years in limbo, it was published at last, those dreams ceased. But time goes on, you think of more and more books you should have written, stories half-fledged and left in the file called "Work in Progress." I know some of these narratives will never be finished. I dream of half-formed, fetal beings, left abandoned on a cold floor. Sometimes they are blackened, like frozen corpses. They take malign forms: I dream of a castle floor, where the children come shrieking through, and so evil are they, that they have the actual capacity of revolting stone, of making the flags shrink away from them. Risen from the ground, they are naked and sexless, foulmouthed and knowing. My impulse is to injure or kill them, swat them like flies, like little demons that, if they're left, will range about the world and will bad-mouth me and misrepresent me and filch from me everything I have.

But then I wake up, chilled, and put out my hands to be sure that surfaces are solid, that my own flesh is still warm. I grope for a pen and write down my dream; when the day has settled around me, the prosaic Surrey light, I take my dream to the keyboard and mince it through a second draft.

Afterlife

Whon we came home from Saudi Arabia, we had various houses. Some of them had minor poltergeists, and one of them was home to a nebulous cat. People less suggestible than me were aware of these anomalous phenomena, rational people who didn't make their living by what they could conjure up; so I feel it's all right to admit that I gave house-room to some ghosts. Ghosts are the tags and rags of everyday life, information you acquire that you don't know what to do with, knowledge that you can't process; they're cards thrown out of your card index, blots on the page. "Ghosts" are whatever it is that moves the furniture, stops the clocks, hides things from you, and arranges for you to be locked out of your hotel room. It's just the little dead, I say to myself, kicking up a fuss, demanding attention by the infantile methods that are the only ones available to them.

We lived first in a tiny flat in Windsor, the castle looming in at the window. Then, to buy space, in a no-man's-land along an arterial road, somewhere outside Slough. At the time we bought Owl Cottage we were living in Sunningdale in a ramshackle flat converted from a former mother-and-baby home, which had been run by nuns.

Drummond House was built of a red brick whose color time didn't soften. By the look of it, it had been put up in the 1890s, with 1920s additions. Its façade was blunt, square, and ugly; the back of the building was tile-hung, like an overgrown cottage, and almost had charm.

After the place had been hacked into flats, there were four households under the one roof, and a poor sort of roof it was; when it rained we had to run around with buckets. The big rooms were gracelessly partitioned, and there were crucifixes and Latin mottoes in unexpected places, and one of the neighbors was spiteful and intractably litigious. But there were compensations; a copper beech behind the house filtered into the rooms, on winter afternoons, a lemon-colored light, and as you lay in the deep Edwardian bathtub, you could hear in the background the reassuring shuffle of branch-line trains. In summer there was a backcloth of shifting, rustling green, green against green, as if the whole world were made of leaves.

We had been seven years in this house. Then, within the space of a few months, it became unbearable. It was a wasting asset, its lease shortening. We decided to sell up to a builder, who would give us the market rate for the flat in return for our deposit on a patch of rutted ground eight miles away, ground on which stood, preconceived but not yet embryonic, a five-bed detached "executive home."

We had looked at the plans of the "executive homes" with fewer bedrooms, but they were dispiriting hutches. "We'll go for the biggest one," we said: five beds and three baths. I can have two offices, I thought, in two of the bedrooms. And think; a spare room with the beds made up tidily, where guests will be en suite and always expected: instead of this ambling around in the small hours with a drink in one hand, a pillowcase in the other, a towel over your shoulder, and the guest trailing behind you, bleating, "Don't go to any trouble." And we'll have a garden that will be—unlike our garden in Sunningdale—attached to the house. And think of the central heating—our own modern controllable system, instead of the monster boiler of Drummond House, housed in its own shed or cave, which demanded each autumn the sacrifice of seven virgins before it would agree to splutter into life and infiltrate a vitiating heat between the whistling drafts.

We spent a nervous summer, thinking that the litigious neighbor would somehow spoil this happy arrangement. In the evenings, we drove over to the building site, where down the hillside spilled walls grown to the height of eight-year-olds. These walls, soon, would be raised up; one evening we stood under the vast gaping skeleton of the roof, looking up at its timbers, arched above us like the ribs of a brontosaurus. On later visits, we climbed into the prerooms, and looked out through the holes where windows would be. We would see other couples, picking their way through the caterpillar tracks in the churned-up earth, between the pipes and cables; we would see the wondering look in their eyes. No one could believe that out of these bits of plastic and concrete the vast solid structures would grow, the structures of family houses, houses for the stable modern families of Middle England.

They were not, our neighbors-to-be, the kind of families whom the breakup statistics comprehend. They were not the sort for adulterous upsets, for drunken fumbles, for spring folie, for subterfuge and lies. They were grounded infotech folk, hardware or software people, bright philistines, sharp and intelligent. They were mobile in their habits till their children fixed them: keen, pragmatic, willing to defer gratification: committed to their offspring, investing in them. Men and wives met each other halfway, gentle fathers and defined, energetic mothers. They were a new sort of people who didn't seem to feel the need of history, personal or collective. They seemed to have sprung straight from a pot in Homebase, putting out glossy, polished leaves; they had parents, but they had them as weekend accessories, appearing on summer Sundays like their barbecue forks. In this part of the world, each family unit runs like a model small business, and the accounts, you may be sure, are squared at the end of each quarter: and if quarter is wanted, a small measure is granted: and if quarter is granted, the favor must be returned: and when the columns are totted they must balance, I think, husband to wife, wife to husband, with none of the shocking deficits that are incurred in the wilder parts of the world.

One evening we drove up to the site and saw that they were putting the façade on our executive home. The drawings had lied to us; we had not been promised this. For some time we sat in our parked car. I may have used some rough language, and said I wanted out of the deal. But my sentiments dried on the air. It was too late. We were committed. After all, I said at last, when you're in it, you don't have to look at it, do you?

We moved in November. They were someone else's problem, the half-timbered elevations from Disneyland, the herringbone "brickwork" that was as thick as cardboard, glued onto the raw building blocks beneath: the fake leaded windows. Our problems, the builders told us brightly, were just what you call "snagging"; for instance, the central heating that creaked and banged, and groaned in the night like a ghoul. Once we had settled in, we were able to relax and appreciate the house's more charming features. The washbasins were specially designed so that the soap slid off them, unless you wedged it behind the tap. The watered-down paint on the walls was so thin that a casual wipe with a cloth would remove it, along with the mark that had offended you.

Summer came. The newly turfed gardens sprouted a mini-estate of multicolored Wendy houses and play shacks, plastic slides and swings and paddling pools. I should like to say that the happy laughter of children drifted in from the gardens, but more often it was their aggrieved wails as they pitched off their climbing frames headfirst, or were beaten up by their brothers and sisters. As I sat in my stifling upstairs room, coaxing out of my computer the novel concealed somewhere in its operating system, I could hear their mothers' voices from below, running the gamut from coaxing to shrieks of fury. I asked myself, why don't they like their children more? Why are they so angry with them for doing childish things? If they hate childhood so much, why didn't they arrange to give birth to adults?

For a year or two in the new house, our possessions expanded to fill the rooms. The cupboards were packed with linen and towels. We bought everything by the dozen. We had bath cleaner by the crate: enough sandwich bags for a primary-school picnic: enough tinfoil to wrap a town hall. Shuttling to and fro between Surrey and Norfolk required lists, master lists and sublists, and constant calculation and recalculation of stocks and supplies. Was everything scrubbed and scoured? Was everything warm? Was every cupboard full to capacity, and everything scraped up to the standard that—God knows why—I had set myself? My husband knew a couple, childless like us, who ate out every night. They kept nothing in their fridge but a bottle of champagne and an inch of souring milk. Imagine, I thought, any woman so deficient in household arts; imagine any man, so wretchedly deprived of pies. Myself, I never peeled two pounds of potatoes if I thought five would do. I would take up a great fistful of spaghetti, and toss it in the boiling pot. I used to think, there's plenty here, for anybody who drops in.

There must have been a moment of realization, though I don't remember it clearly: a moment when I looked at the contents of the cupboards and said, but who is all this for? Who am I expecting? I knew, if I thought about it, that I was expecting the unborn. But could I face them anymore? Perhaps I'd grown away from them, without noticing it, over the years. One day, when I was upstairs in one of my two offices, listening to my best bit of Telemann, the merry, jingling ice-cream van lurched around the corner playing: "The Teddy Bears' Picnic."

I left my desk and fell into my armchair; a chair which (like many of our chairs) could be pulled out to form a spare bed. Bugger off teddy bears, I said: hugging myself, my head drooping. Off back to the woods where unless I'm much mistaken, you're in for a big surprise. I was angry, unreasonably so. I felt I had been invaded by the juvenile, my attention trashed. What would I do if real children came padding at the door, smiling their sticky smiles, smearing my printout with sticky hands, and pressing DELETE on my keyboard? I could have coped once, of course; I'd have found a way to laugh about it. I'd have said they were my inspiration, that I'd be only half a woman without them. But that was then, when I was twenty-five, in the days when, notionally anyway, I was fertile. Now I was tired, more fragile, less tolerant. I stood up, closed the window, put the Telemann on again, and sat down at my desk.

Then a thing occurred to me, about ghost children. They don't age, unless you make them. They don't age, so they don't know it's time to leave home. They won't, without a struggle, be kicked out of your psyche. They will hang on by every means they know; they won't agree to go, until you make your intentions very clear. They're stupid, so it's not enough to tell them; you have to show them as well.

I went round to my next-door neighbor. "You know you said, if we were ever selling the house, that we should tell you before we told anyone else?"

Oh, wow, said my neighbor. You're going, are you?

Come over, I said, when the children get home. Have a look around. Think where everything would go. At four o'clock they came in a gang. The children whooped through the rooms. They couldn't wait to evict us. Only the three-year-old cried, sobbing, "When do we swap the pets?" for she thought that we were exchanging houses and all their contents, and that she had to give up her white rabbit for the cat who was steadily hating her from a bookshelf, thinking which way to prey on her would be best. Once we knew her mistake, we soon ironed it out, soothed her temper. That evening, over a bottle of wine, we shook hands on the deal. Our "second home" must go as well, we decide. If we're going to remake our lives, we must do the job properly.

It is August 12, 2000: a Sunday in Norfolk. We are taking Owl Cottage apart. My eldest brother and my husband carry out the pine table, which I remember as my first purchase for the Windsor flat. I remember working at that table, when it was new and smooth as glass, the sash windows flung open to spring sunshine, the kitchen smelling of daffodils and chopped onions; and a few trial words going down on paper, words scented with furniture polish. I have a nervous sort of nostalgia for any surface I have written a book on, or even half a book; I think the words, for better or worse, have sunk into the grain of the wood. But the pine table is bashed and battered now, its surface gouged and its legs wobbling; I am touched by fellow feeling. I pat it for the last time: good table, good table. I don't watch it leave the house. It's going to a good home in my brother's workshop: light duties, an honorable retirement.

Owl Cottage sold within an hour of going on the market. One of Mr. Ewing's ladies rang, her voice astonished, to say, were we happy to accept the asking price? I have never had anything before or since, that another person wanted so much. And as we pack up, we are rushed, a little flustered; we hadn't thought we would have to quit so soon.

My mother arrives. Now we are going to do something difficult, which is to clear the loft. Some boxes were stowed up there by Jack when my parents first arrived in the county, and left there; now no one can remember what is in them.

When I went to Africa, I left a box of my own in the eaves of my parents' house. In it was my *Complete Works of Shakespeare*, which they had bought me (to keep me quiet) when I was ten. Even when it was new it was cheap; but what did I care? It was bound in fraying black cloth, its paper was yellowing and woody, its blurred type looked as if it were running from the page; I loved that book. My child's fingerprints were on every leaf of it. I felt as if it talked back to me, as if I had exchanged breath with it; no other *Complete Works* would ever be the same. By the time I was leaving England the book was nearly fifteen years old, it was falling apart, its glue drying, its pages brittle; I still liked it too much to trust it to sea freight. I knew that to pack it in my suitcase—a book like a house brick, against my allowance of 20 kg—would be a little ridiculous. Besides, I feared the effects on it of a change of climate. "I'll just store it in the eaves," I said, for the eaves were spacious, dry, and cool. In the box, also, was a bibliography for my French Revolution book, kept in a humble school exercise book with a stiff burgundy cover. I thought—

and I was right—that it wouldn't be much use to me where I was going.

Three years later—around the time I went to St. George's to have my insides remodeled—I came back to my parents' house to reclaim the box. The Revolution book was with a publisher, and if it was accepted I would need my bibliography, to help me with editing and checking. I felt a sober, righteous pleasure as I waited for it to emerge from the eaves, and I anticipated opening my Shakespeare, wondering which passage I would light on first. But the searchers drew a blank. They frowned, puzzled, and rubbed out of their hair the fine dust of accreted pigeon droppings. It must be in there somewhere, they said. They dived in again, bent double, and emerged rubbing their backs, shaking their heads. No box, no Shakespeare, nothing at all conforming to the description of a burgundy notebook with five years of my reading life in it. "Oh, look again," I begged. They did; they drew a blank. The family said, that's strange. Where oh where can Ilary's box be? Some suggested supernatural reasons for its disappearance. But I had my own theory. Shakespeare is bunk. History is bunk. Why are women always smiling? Smile, smile, smile.

So much for my box; now at Owl Cottage, Jack's boxes come down from the loft, the men's feet bouncing on the steel ladder. The boxes are heavy, covered in what looks like iron filings. We take them into the kitchen and wipe them down. One box contains a tidy stack of *National Geographic* magazines. We know the contents before we open it, because it is precisely labeled in Jack's fading hand. Another box seems to be full of old engineering textbooks. Why keep them, I wonder? But it's not for me to judge the quality of someone else's nostalgia. It is five years since his death. Soon after the funeral my mother packed up his watercolor paints, ready for me to use, at some unlikely date when I have the leisure. We framed what we could from his last sketchbook, anything that was nearly complete: sea, sand, clouds. We put the sketchbook away with the paints, and with it the pictures he must have been working on: another seascape, and what may be, emerging from the paper's weave, an apple tree under a darkening sky.

"Get another cloth," I say. "There's a whole big box of them, under the sink." The textbooks—sad wastepaper—we pile in a stack. Then out comes an edition of Creasey's *Decisive Battles,* which I gave Jack because of its fine binding and marbled endpapers—and which, surprisingly, he decided to read. Now comes—I laugh as it emerges—an ancient, grimy relic called *"An Analysis of English History:* with Appendix and Maps." I pick it out of the box; as I try to open it, its pages fall like loose cards into my hand. Inside the cover is written BERYL A WHITE, 58 BANKBOTTOM, HADFIELD, NEAR MANCHESTER, ENGLAND. Beryl, my heroine, my cousin after whom I named my pointy-headed doll! I shuffle the pages, I look at a few. Their content is only slightly familiar; but is this not the tale of my native land? The story begins in the days when all the main players are called Ethel, those days when the successor of Ethelfrith marries Ethelburga, daughter of Ethelbert: hilarious consequences ensue. I shuffle the pages again: "War with France: this war arose from an unseemly jest." Shuffle again: "The skeletons of two children were found buried at the foot of a staircase . . . Marlborough took the field, but owing to the extreme dilatoriness of the Dutch . . ." The book—if it can be called a book, in its loose-leaf state—is full of moral judgments, against unseemly jesting and turning up late for the fight. King John died of a fever brought on by anxiety, which one sees was weak of him; the character of Mary Tudor, naturally mild, took a turn for the worse "when she gave her hand to the Spaniard."

I put down the Analysis regretfully, vowing I will get back to it. Here is another book of Beryl's, her name in pencil in a round baby hand. "She must have it back," my mother says. "I'll keep it for her." It is "Alice"—both adventures—in a jacket of porridge-colored canvas. Next—but why?—comes a copy of *Lorna Doone,* abridged for the young. It is the remnant of a set of miscellaneous nineteenth-century novels I had for Christmas, perhaps the year I was ten. The colophon is a silhouette of a man in a tall hat, holding by the hand a silhouette child; the publisher's name is Dean & Son. How has this one survived, when *Treasure Island* has gone, the only one of the set to have a yellow jacket; where is *Jane Eyre,* bound in dull green? I remember the first time I read *Jane Eyre:* probably every woman writer does, because you recognize, when you have hardly begun it, that you are reading a story about yourself. The books with their colored bindings were passed on, down the family; I remember how my youngest brother liked *Children of the New Forest.* It had a peach-colored binding; I thought it was tedious, myself. *Kidnapped* came in dark blue. I knew by heart its opening lines, and running through my memory, the words still affect me with a shiver of trepidation: "I will begin the story of my adventures with a certain morning early in the month of June, the year of grace 1751, when I took the key for the last time out of the door of my father's house." Like a wimp, like a girl, I wanted David Balfour to stay at home, with the kindly minister Mr. Campbell, with his dead parents who lay in the churchyard under the rowan trees. The plot would never have got beyond its second page, if it had stood to me: its hero would never have left Essendean. I loved and trusted Alan Breck, his bantam swagger, his defiance of logic and the odds; but I worried about David and his welfare, much more than I worried about Jane Eyre, who, in my opinion, had stitched Rochester's eyes shut long before he went blind.

It is summer at Owl Cottage; light bounces on the black-and-white tiles of the kitchen floor. I put my arms, briefly, around the shoulders of my mother and my brother's wife. The box we are dipping into seems deeper than we thought, darker and fustier. Almost at the bottom of it, we find one of Jack's own books—one of those that came with him when he moved into our house at Brosscroft. It is *Out with Romany*, its title almost illegible now, its cover, which I remember as green, now faded to gray. It is illustrated with naïve woodcuts: a hedgehog, a bird's nest, hares dancing. We pass it from hand to hand. I'd like it, says my brother's wife, I like these pictures. "Yes, take it, love," my mother says. Then last of all comes the vast tome of Tennyson, square and brown like a well-packed parcel, like a parcel that has been left in a sorting office for thirty years. I open it, and the odor of decay rises up, so powerful and bitter that it seems like the smell of burning. For a moment I stand, shaken, recalling this book in my child's hands: it was old then, the pages freckled with butter-colored marks. "Can I have this?" I ask. "It must be middle age, you know, but I've been wanting to reread Tennyson lately." I open the book, and my fingertips turn gray as I leaf through it.

> *When cats run home and light is come,*
> *And dew is cold upon the ground . . .*

My mother, standing next to me, brushes my elbow; silently, heads bent over the empty box, we begin to cry.

October 2000: moving day at last. The sales of our two houses have been tied up neatly, completion of both on the same morning. Owl Cottage has been packed up by removal men; I couldn't stand to do it myself, to turn the key for the last time and leave Jack's baffled spirit locked in the shell of the house. At our Disneyland villa, as our furniture vanishes into the removal van, our neighbors, their children and their friends spread out over the garden, brooms and vacuum cleaners held like bayonets across their chests, ready for the charge. They have taken down a fence panel between the two gardens to give themselves access; as soon as the phone rings, as soon as the word from the lawyers comes through, they storm down the slope of the lawn and pour through the French windows, mob-handed. I have to plead for a safe corner in the house, for a twenty-minute respite, till the cats and I can be collected, for we are going last. I sit on the bathroom floor, the door locked against the mob, waiting, the minutes ebbing away, talking to the cats to soothe them, while they fume and moan in their traveling cages and rattle the bars. By the time I come downstairs, and walk out of the front door for the last time, the neighbors have got their furniture in place, their milk in the fridge, their food in the cupboards. It is theirs already, and they fit it; I cannot believe this house ever belonged to me. It has four children in it; solid, squalling, overexcited, ready for a showdown about who gets which room. The cats shake their fists at them, and curse as I hand over the spare door keys: as the tailgate of the car slams on their bawling, the house becomes history.

The place we live in now is an apartment in a converted lunatic asylum. It was built in the 1860s, one of a loop of great institutions flung around London to catch and contain its burgeoning mad population, the melancholic and the syphilitic, the damaged and the deluded, the people who had forgotten their manners and the people who had forgotten their names.

Aren't you afraid of ghosts? visitors say. But I smile and shake my head; I say, not I. Not I: not here: not now.

We are on the top floor; but a spiral staircase leads even higher, to a small square room in the clock tower. We are the keepers of the gargoyles that guard the roofs, and we have a long view over the country, over the city of Guildford, dropped into the landscape like an egg into a dish: to a distant, fuzzy line of uplands that, on rainy days, when cloud thickens and almost obscures it, I can easily imagine is the moorland of my childhood.

Two wings of the old building have been preserved and converted, but thousands of houses have been built on the asylum's land. It is hard to believe that seven years ago it was open fields. An elderly man who grew up in the district told me what this countryside was like, before the mechanical diggers moved in. It was an area of market gardens and plant nurseries, and open land cut up with streams and ditches, into which, when he was a boy and out rabbiting, he would invariably fall; and pick his way home, at twilight, half-drowned and dripping, to be shouted at by his mother. He was a good talker, and I found myself sliding, in imagination, into the country that he had shown me, so that it became a part of my own terrain.

Now on light clear nights, I sometimes go out onto the balcony; the clock face hangs above me like a second moon, lighting up the flickering tongues of the gargoyles, stone saurians leaning out into darkness and space. It is quiet up here: except for the background purr of traveling cars, on the circular road that holds the new houses, the new families, in a loose, careless embrace. I wrap myself in a blanket, and rest my forehead on the balcony's freezing rail, and think about what I have lost and what I have gained. For me, the balcony is the best thing about the asylum. I am out there in all weathers, looking over the army land that is the last remnant of the unpopulated place this used to be. Sometimes, at dawn or at dusk, I pick out from the gloom—I think I do—a certain figure, traversing those rutted fields in a hushed and pearly light, picking a way among the treacherous rivulets and the concealed ditches. It is a figure shrouded in a cloak, bearing certain bulky objects wrapped in oilcloth, irregular in shape: not heavy but awkward to carry. This figure is me; these shapes, hidden in their wrappings, are books that, God willing, I am going to write. But when was God ever willing? And what is this dim country, what is this tenuous path I lose so often—where am I trying to get to, when the light is so uncertain? Steps to literature, I think; I have tottered one or two. I move back from the window, dawn or dusk; I think of other houses, which seem not so long ago.

At 20 Brosscroft, the windows printed on our curtains are alight from within, their flowerpots spilling scarlet blooms, the candle flames swelling, flickering boldly against the fading northern afternoon. The table is laid, and the dead are peering at their place cards, and shuffling into their chairs, and shaking out their napkins, waiting, expectant, for whatever is next. Food or entertainment, it's all one to the eyeless, the shriveled and the thin: to the ones who have crossed into the land where only the living can provide their light. I will always look after you, I want to say, however long you have been gone. I will always feed you, and try to keep you entertained; and you must do the same for me. This is your daughter Ilary speaking, and this is her book.

About the Author

Hilary Mantel is the critically acclaimed author of eight novels, including *The Giant, O'Brien; A Change of Climate;* and *Eight Months on Ghazzah Street*. Winner of the Hawthornden Prize, she reviews for *The New York Times* and *The New York Review of Books* and lives in England.